T0146137

# Evaluating the Effectiveness of Artificial Intelligence Systems in Intelligence Analysis

DANIEL ISH, JARED ETTINGER, CHRISTOPHER FERRIS

Prepared for the Office of the Secretary of Defense
Approved for public release; distribution unlimited

NATIONAL DEFENSE RESEARCH INSTITUTE

For more information on this publication, visit **www.rand.org/t/RRA464-1**.

## About RAND

The RAND Corporation is a research organization that develops solutions to public policy challenges to help make communities throughout the world safer and more secure, healthier and more prosperous. RAND is nonprofit, nonpartisan, and committed to the public interest. To learn more about RAND, visit www.rand.org.

## Research Integrity

Our mission to help improve policy and decisionmaking through research and analysis is enabled through our core values of quality and objectivity and our unwavering commitment to the highest level of integrity and ethical behavior. To help ensure our research and analysis are rigorous, objective, and nonpartisan, we subject our research publications to a robust and exacting quality-assurance process; avoid both the appearance and reality of financial and other conflicts of interest through staff training, project screening, and a policy of mandatory disclosure; and pursue transparency in our research engagements through our commitment to the open publication of our research findings and recommendations, disclosure of the source of funding of published research, and policies to ensure intellectual independence. For more information, visit www.rand.org/about/principles.

RAND's publications do not necessarily reflect the opinions of its research clients and sponsors.

# Preface

This research develops methodologies for understanding the mission impact of deploying artificial intelligence (AI) systems to support intelligence missions as a function of the performance achieved by the system. A two-pronged approach is pursued, with a general framework enabling qualitative analysis and a supplemental model of a particular class of systems with quantitative results. Our results underscore the importance of critically assessing how the performance of AI systems is measured and tailoring the metrics chosen to the function the system will perform.

The research reported here was completed in March 2021 and underwent security review with the sponsor and the Defense Office of Prepublication and Security Review before public release.

This research was sponsored by the Office of the Secretary of Defense and conducted within the Cyber and Intelligence Policy Center of the RAND National Security Research Division (NSRD), which operates the RAND National Defense Research Institute (NDRI), a federally funded research and development center (FFRDC) sponsored by the Office of the Secretary of Defense, the Joint Staff, the Unified Combatant Commands, the Navy, the Marine Corps, the defense agencies, and the defense intelligence enterprise.

For more information on the RAND Cyber and Intelligence Center, see www.rand.org/nsrd/intel or contact the director (contact information is provided on the webpage).

# Contents

# Figures and Tables

## Figures

## Tables

# Summary

The intelligence community (IC) and Department of Defense (DoD) have shown interest in developing and deploying artificial intelligence (AI) systems to support intelligence analysis, both as an opportunity to leverage new technology and as a solution for a data glut. This glut, which stems from a proliferation of data that defies human processing alone, is a particularly acute problem for certain intelligence disciplines. However, previous studies at the RAND Corporation, along with studies and strategies published by public organizations, have identified validation, verification, testing, and evaluation (VVT&E) as a central challenge complicating the deployment of AI systems in a national security context.

We focus on one portion of the VVT&E problem: identifying metrics (alternatively, measures of performance) for AI systems that are adapted to the mission at hand. Using the academic AI literature, intelligence literature, and informal interviews with subject-matter experts across RAND and the government, this study develops a methodology for assessing the impact an AI system is likely to have on the intelligence mission that it supports and traces those impacts back to the properties of the system itself. Both the calculated impact and the metrics that predict it can then be used to characterize the performance of the AI system in a way that informs decisionmakers as to the actual value of the system to the mission.

Though replicating human performance is sometimes cited as a sufficient criterion for success for an AI system and the most relevant threshold to cross before deploying a system, we argue that the applicability of this criterion is much narrower than it might initially appear.

Additionally, even within the scope of its applicability, this standard is more limiting than a full accounting of system impact, since it provides only a minimum standard and not an understanding of the positive value the system might provide or how to optimally distribute this value.

In this report, we organize our analysis of AI systems by how well they support the next step in the intelligence process. Since we need a conceptual model for the process into which the AI system will be inserted in order to determine what the "next step" after the AI system is, we adopt the intelligence cycle as a model for the intelligence process. We define a set of four "system function categories" that are organized in part by the intelligence cycle and divide the functions of AI systems that support intelligence based on the properties of the "next step" they support (see Table S.1). Put another way, these system function categories bin AI systems by how their output is utilized. The

**Table S.1**
**System Function Categories**

|  | Evaluation Support | Automated Analysis | Information Prioritization | Collection Support |
|---|---|---|---|---|
| Description | Ingests reports or products to determine their quality and their alignment with priorities | Transforms or enriches data without human supervision | Ingests available information and analyst preferences to connect analysts with useful information | Ingests available information to direct future collections |
| Example | A tool that classifies reports according to National Intelligence Priorities Framework (NIPF) and tracks which priorities are being adequately collected on | A tool that transcribes, translates, and summarizes signals intelligence (SIGINT) | A recommender that flags reports for all source analysts based on previous interests or ratings | A system that uses SIGINT to direct imagery intelligence (IMINT) to find or track a target |

NOTE: Examples are artificial/notional and do not necessarily reflect actual systems.

way the output is to be utilized provides a natural platform to analyze the consequences of errors in system output, which we can then trace back to understand how different error rates connect to different magnitudes of consequences at this "next step." For information prioritization and collection support, we find that this procedure yields ways of reasoning about the impact of such systems without grappling with the difficult questions of how intelligence and the actions selected by decisionmakers contribute to the overall security of the United States. For the two other categories, we find that obstacles to this sort of detailed analysis of absolute efficacy remain, though workable baseline performance standards can be deduced.

We then develop a simple mathematical model for the operation of an information prioritization system that captures the consequences of errors on the part of systems that perform this function and use it to derive general results about the impact of such a system in terms of analyst time and the probability of missing a piece of relevant information. To construct this model, we analyze the two errors that such a system can make: incorrectly prioritizing (false positive) and incorrectly de-prioritizing (false negative) a piece of information. In the case of a false positive, we find that the cost of such errors to be quantifiable in terms of the impingement on the overall budget of analyst time without meaningful return. In the case of false negatives, on the other hand, we argue that it is difficult to defensibly assign a cost to them. To avoid this difficulty, we construct a model that predicts the residual risk of false negatives as a function of the amount of time the analyst spends using the system. Put another way, the model predicts the "return on investment" of analyst time mediated by the properties of the system.

We then demonstrate the utility of this model in a few artificial examples. First, we show that this model demonstrates the criticality of developing metrics properly matched with actual system usage by exhibiting an example where the model shows that a system with lower mathematical accuracy happens to be of greater utility for information prioritization than one with greater accuracy. This theme is then extended to the model itself, as we demonstrate that different systems can be preferable depending on the amount of analyst time available to review the output. We then demonstrate how this model can be used to optimize the degree to which the information prioritization system errs on the side of false positives or false negatives by tuning the threshold at which the system marks an item as useful. Under most conditions, this optimal threshold results in the system marking precisely as many items useful as the analyst can actually review. With this tuning accomplished, the model provides the promised return on investment on analyst time (see Figure S.1), a valuable input for strategy for decisionmakers.

When combined with existing results from the AI and intelligence literature, the study of this model furnishes two general conclusions pertaining to the efficacy of AI systems supporting intelligence:

- **Using metrics not matched to actual priorities obscures system performance and impedes informed choice of the optimal**

**Figure S.1**
**Percentage of Useful Items Found as a Function of Review Capacity**

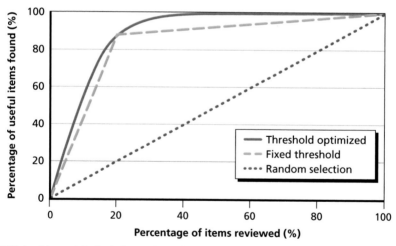

NOTE: In this model, the Information Prioritization system marks all items as either useful or not useful, and the analyst then reviews a fixed percentage of the items that have arrived, shown on the x-axis. The fixed threshold corresponds to a single possible system with an arbitrarily chosen threshold. Each point on the threshold-optimized curve represents the performance of the system optimized for that review percentage. More detail can be found in Chapter Three.

**system.** Metrics are not necessarily meaningful in a vacuum, and decisionmakers should anticipate needing to do work to develop ways of measuring system performance that match their priorities. Since the metrics typically used to capture the performance of a system do not all agree on which of a pair of systems is performing better, simply choosing a metric arbitrarily will not enable decisionmakers to rank systems by how useful they will be to the mission the system supports. Similarly, engineering decisions ranging from overall model design to the optimization of the trade between false positives and false negatives are made to maximize system performance with respect to the metric of record. Metric choice should take place *before* the system is built and be guided by attempts to estimate the real impact of system deployment.

- **Effectiveness, and therefore the metrics that measure it, can depend not just on system properties, but on how the system is used.** In the case of information prioritization systems, this is captured by the dependence of the number of useful items found on the amount of time an analyst spends reviewing the output of the system. Since the optimal system is necessarily the most effective, this also means that which system is optimal can depend on how the system is used. For instance, in the context of information prioritization systems, different review percentages can result in different determinations as to which of a pair of systems is preferable. That is, for a given pair of systems, which system is more effective can depend on how much of the system output can be reviewed. On an engineering level this affects the optimal trade-off between false positives and false negatives. However, both for the question of understanding the effectiveness of a system and that of choosing the optimal system, these are simply examples of more general lessons. When deploying a system, decisionmakers should understand that choices about how the system is used may affect outcomes in concert with the properties of the system itself. Chief among these is the amount of resources devoted to the mission *outside* those devoted to building the system.

Based on this analysis, we make the following recommendations for DoD and IC.

**Begin with the right metrics.** When considering acquiring an AI system, DoD and IC should begin by developing a detailed understanding of the way this system will be utilized and choosing metrics that reflect success with respect to this utilization. For information prioritization AI systems in particular, we recommend a version of the information prioritization performance model, possibly adapted and extended to cover the precise case at hand. Through this process, AI system acquirers can understand what the impact of the performance achieved by system designers will be. AI system designers will also benefit from the clear objective guiding their engineering decisions and will deliver a more effective AI system if this objective is aligned with user priorities.

**Reevaluate (and retune) regularly.** Since the world around the AI system continues to evolve after deployment, AI system evaluation must continue as a portion of regular maintenance. Narrowly, this means continuing to assemble test data and measure the performance of the AI system to detect any changes in performance. More broadly, this must include reevaluations of the deployment context of the system. Is the AI system still being used in the way first envisioned when it was deployed? Is the same amount of resources being devoted to utilizing the output of the system and accomplishing the mission the system is meant to support? As these details change, the right way to measure effectiveness may shift. At the most dramatic, this might result in entirely different metrics from those that were used to evaluate the system at deployment becoming most appropriate. In addition, the AI system might need to be retuned (e.g., to a different balance between false positives and false negatives) to reflect the changing priorities of users.

**Speak the language.** System designers have a well-established set of metrics typically used to capture the performance of AI systems. Though new metrics can be constructed, being conversant in these traditional metrics will ease communication with experts during the process of designing a new system or maintaining an existing one. Ensure that coursework for acquisition professionals who may acquire AI systems provides an introduction to these traditional metrics. Additionally, acquisition professionals would benefit from an understanding of the assumptions and reasoning that underlie the statistical approach to evaluating these systems, which could also be included in the relevant coursework. More broadly, a common resource on metrics for AI systems should be created or identified that can serve as a common touchpoint across IC.

**Further research is needed into methods of evaluating AI system effectiveness.** In addition to representing a step forward for assessing the effectiveness of AI systems supporting intelligence, this effort serves as a demonstration of what is lost when well-tuned methods of assessing this effectiveness are not present. Unfortunately, further basic research is needed to provide these methods across all the systems and deployment contexts pertinent to intelligence missions. This research is distinct from the considerable effort rightly directed toward developing methodologies for assuring the integrity and reliability of AI systems for defense and intelligence applications. In addition to being able to assure that these systems will not suddenly stop working at a critical juncture, we must be able to critically assess whether they will enhance effectiveness in the mission they support at all when judged not just by a narrow definition of their task but by the actual value they provide. Put another way, research is needed to actually understand the contours of the upside for such systems, in addition to understanding how to guard against downsides. At present, for intelligence in particular, the results of this effort indicate that room for improvement remains in methodologies for assessing the actual value provided to users by these systems.

# Acknowledgments

We are grateful for the time, support, and valuable insights provided by colleagues both inside and outside RAND Corporation. Outside RAND, we wish to thank Barry Zulaf at the Office of the Director of National Intelligence; Jeff Alstott, Carl Rubino, and Timothy McKinnon at Intelligence Advanced Research Projects Activity; and Jon Fiscus and Jim Horan at the National Institute for Standards and Technology for their generosity, time, and perspective. At RAND, we wish to thank Lance Menthe, Matt Walsh, Eric Landree, Rich Girven, Brad Knopp, Mark Cozad, Jon Fujiwara, Michael Shurkin, Anthony Vassalo, Gavin Hartnett, and Zach Haldeman for their time and tremendously helpful input and guidance. Finally, we thank Lance Menthe and Drew Lohn for their thoughtful and thorough review of a draft of this report. The views expressed herein are our own, and any errors or shortcomings in this report are solely our responsibility.

# Abbreviations

| | |
|---|---|
| AI | artificial intelligence |
| AIM | Augmenting Intelligence Using Machines |
| BETTER | Better Extraction from Text Towards Enhanced Retrieval |
| CAUSE | Cyber-Attack Automated Unconventional Sensor Environment |
| CIA | Central Intelligence Agency |
| CORE3D | Creation of Operationally Realistic 3D Environment |
| DIVA | Deep Intermodal Video Analytics |
| DoD | Department of Defense |
| FELIX | Finding Engineering-Linked Indicators |
| Fun GCAT | Functional Genomic and Computational Assessment of Threats |
| GEOINT | geospatial intelligence |
| GIS | Geographic Information System |
| HFC | Hybrid Forecasting Competition |
| HUMINT | human intelligence |
| IARPA | Intelligence Advanced Research Projects Activity |
| IC | intelligence community |
| IMINT | imagery intelligence |
| JAIC | Joint Artificial Intelligence Council |

| | |
|---|---|
| MATERIAL | Machine Translation for English Retrieval of Information in Any Language |
| ML | machine learning |
| NGA | National Geospatial-Intelligence Agency |
| NIPF | National Intelligence Priorities Framework |
| NLP | natural language processing |
| NSCAI | National Security Council on Artificial Intelligence |
| ODNI | Office of the Director of National Intelligence |
| OSI | open-source indicators |
| SIGINT | signals intelligence |
| VVT&E | validation, verification, testing, and evaluation |

# CHAPTER ONE

# Introduction

The Office of the Director of National Intelligence (ODNI) chief technology adviser, Dean Souleles, stated in July 2020 that "in our increasingly complex digital world, the IC [intelligence community] must adapt and adopt AI [artificial intelligence] and related technologies to carry out its critical mission."[1] Former Deputy Associate Director of the Central Intelligence Agency (CIA) for Learning, Joseph Gartin, wrote in June 2019 that

> the field of intelligence analysis is at an inflection point. Behind us, several decades of accomplishment and innovation, chastened at times by errors and shaped by cautious incrementalism. Ahead, a future—as in all knowledge industries—still coming into view but shaped by the powerful and potentially disruptive effects of artificial intelligence, big data, and machine learning.[2]

In August 2018, the National Security Commission on Artificial Intelligence (NSCAI) was created to "consider the methods and means necessary to advance the development of artificial intelligence, machine learning, and associated technologies to comprehensively address the national security needs of the United States."[3] The 2019 ODNI Aug-

---

[1] Office of the Director of National Intelligence (ODNI), "Intelligence Community Releases Artificial Intelligence Principles and Framework," press release, Washington, D.C., July 23, 2020.

[2] Joseph W. Gartin, "The Future of Analysis," *Studies in Intelligence*, Vol. 63, No. 2, Extracts, June 2019, p. 1.

[3] National Security Commission on Artificial Intelligence, "About," webpage, undated.

menting Intelligence using Machines (AIM) Initiative notes that "the pace at which data are generated . . . is increasing exponentially and long ago exceeded our collective ability to understand it or to find the most relevant data with which to make analytic judgments." It declares that AI is "crucial for future mission success and efficiency" and that it poses both an opportunity to leverage new technology and a solution for a data glut.[4]

Indeed, too much data collected can make finding the right data challenging. As intelligence expert Mark Lowenthal aptly notes, "If you have more haystacks, you do not necessarily get more needles."[5] IC confronts a large, and growing, haystack. Speaking at the National Geospatial Intelligence Symposium in 2017, then National Geospatial-Intelligence Agency (NGA) Director Robert Cardillo stated:

> If we were to attempt to manually exploit the commercial satellite imagery, we expect to have over the next 20 years, we would need eight million imagery analysts. Even now, every day in just one combat theater with a single sensor, we collect the data equivalent of three NFL [National Football League] seasons—every game. In high definition![6]

Cardillo's statement suggests that even within specific intelligence types, such as imagery intelligence (IMINT) or signals intelligence (SIGINT), the challenge of humans alone processing and making sense of the overwhelming amount of data is likely insurmountable.

This is not to say that IC is uniformly challenged by an over-abundance of data. Data saturation seems to apply in varying degrees depending on the mission and function the intelligence analysis supports. For example, an intelligence analyst focusing on specific high-value targets of a terrorist group or a human intelligence (HUMINT)

---

[4]   ODNI, "The AIM Initiative: A Strategy for Augmenting Intelligence Using Machines," *ODNI Report*, January 16, 2019, p. iv.

[5]   Mark M. Lowenthal, *Intelligence: From Secrets to Policy*, 8th ed., Washington, D.C: Sage, Congressional Quarterly Press, 2020, p. 73.

[6]   Remarks as prepared for Robert Cardillo, Director National Geospatial-Intelligence Agency, June 5, 2017.

counterintelligence analyst focusing on a particular set of assets might not be as overwhelmed as the analysts confronting the aforementioned flood of satellite imagery or even overwhelmed at all. The point is simply that IC is faced with the problem of sifting through massive streams of data and that it has, quite reasonably, identified deploying AI systems as a promising method to address this problem.

This deployment presents a challenge, however. IC must carry out its mission in an uncertain world with a constrained budget. Ideally, IC needs to understand the risks and benefits of any AI system it deploys in the context of the intelligence mission it will support and the way it will be utilized. That is, IC needs to be able to assess the actual benefit provided by an AI system to determine whether, for example, funds would be better spent increasing the number of personnel with language, analytical, and cultural expertise than developing a sophisticated algorithm to sift through social media data. Furthermore, IC needs to understand the efficacy of these AI systems in order to understand how much to rely on them. For example, hypothetically, if most imagery intelligence is only ever processed by a machine, how should we interpret a lack of imagery intelligence supporting an assessment based on other intelligence streams? Surely the answer depends on how reliable the system processing imagery intelligence is. Put another way, while the systems enabled by AI technology are impressive, they are not perfect. As with all systems, IC must understand how effective they are in order to determine how to use them.

We are by no means the first to point out the need for a robust and effective way of measuring the effectiveness of AI systems. Challenges around AI validation, verification, testing, and evaluation (VVT&E) were also identified in RAND's 2019 report on *The Department of Defense Posture for Artificial Intelligence.* That report stated that the "current state of AI VVT&E is nowhere close to ensuring the performance and safety of AI applications" and that "performance metrics optimized for commercial applications are often misaligned with DoD [Department of Defense] needs."[7] The RAND report found that DoD AI strategy and

[7] Danielle C. Tarraf, William Shelton, Edward Parker, Brien Alkire, Diana Gehlhaus, Justin Grana, Alexis Levedahl, Jasmin Leveille, Jared Mondschein, James Ryseff et al., *The*

service AI annexes lacked baselines, metrics, or quantifiable measures to assess progress toward their vision.[8] In June 2019, "The National Artificial Intelligence Research and Development Strategic Plan," produced by the National Science and Technology Council, found that

> standard metrics are needed to define quantifiable measures in order to characterize AI technologies, including but not limited to: accuracy, complexity, trust and competency, risk and uncertainty, explainability, unintended bias, comparison to human performance, and economic impact.[9]

More recently, the July 2020 second-quarter NCSAI report noted that "significant work is needed to establish what appropriate metrics should be to assess system performance across attributes for responsible AI and across profiles for particular applications/contexts."[10]

While these findings relate largely to DoD, the need to identify the right ways to measure the performance and effectiveness of AI systems has also been acknowledged within IC. According to the June 2020 "Artificial Intelligence Ethics Framework for the Intelligence Community," IC personnel are encouraged to ask the right questions for procuring, managing, using, building, protecting, and deploying AI systems. Specifically, when it comes to balancing desired results versus acceptable risk, the framework suggests asking these questions:

> What performance metrics best suit the AI system, such as accuracy, precision, and recall, based on risks determined by mission managers, analysts, and consumers given the potential risks; and how will the accuracy of the information be provided to each of

---

*Department of Defense Posture for Artificial Intelligence: Assessment and Recommendations,* Santa Monica, Calif.: RAND Corporation, RR-4229-OSD, 2019, p. 35.

[8]   Tarraf et al., 2019.

[9]   National Science and Technology Council, Select Committee on Artificial Intelligence, "The National Artificial Intelligence Research and Development Strategic Plan: 2019 Update," June 2019, p. 34.

[10]   National Security Commission on Artificial Intelligence, "Second Quarter Recommendations," *Quarterly Series,* No. 2, July 2020, p. 108.

those stakeholders? What impacts could false positive and false negative rates have on system performance, mission goals, and affected targets of the analysis?[11]

The 2019 AIM Initiative also laments that "too many AI/ML [machine learning] projects launch without metrics to allow the IC to understand whether the investment is on track to succeed or fail."[12]

Unfortunately, choosing the right metrics to assess the effectiveness of an AI system based on the intelligence mission it supports and the way it will be deployed is easier said than done. As alluded to in the AI Ethics Framework, a number of standard ways of characterizing AI system performance exist, including metrics commonly referred to as "precision," "recall," and "accuracy." These metrics measure the performance of the AI system "in a vacuum," without reference to the impact that the AI system has on the mission it supports. That is, though it is immediately clear that more accuracy is better, it is not necessarily clear what level of accuracy is sufficient, since accuracy is not, in and of itself, the goal of the AI system. Rather, the goal of the AI system is the success of the intelligence mission that the AI system supports. In the absence of a clear "exchange rate" between accuracy and intelligence mission success, we can make only ad hoc judgments about what level of performance is sufficient for the intelligence mission.

In addition to the difficulty this issue adds to the problem of establishing minimum standards of performance, the lack of an obvious relationship between standard AI system measures of performance and effectiveness in supporting the intelligence mission complicates the problem of choosing a set of metrics in the first place. A great many ways of measuring this performance exist and necessarily measure the performance of the AI system in different ways. Consequently, not all metrics will agree on which AI system is performing better. Choosing a metric without a direct relationship to actual mission success might result in a misunderstanding of the actual effectiveness of

---

[11] ODNI, "Artificial Intelligence Ethics Framework for the Intelligence Community," v. 1.0, June 2020.

[12] ODNI, 2019, p. 11.

the system, perhaps resulting either in deploying an AI system that is not performing adequately or discarding an AI system that is. Thus, even at the level of choosing how to measure the performance of an AI system, information about how standard metrics of performance connect with AI system effectiveness is necessary to make the decision in an informed manner.

This report aims to begin closing this gap by identifying the ways in which AI systems produce effects in different contexts supporting intelligence and connecting those positive and negative effects with the properties of the AI system itself. That is, this report addresses the question "How are AI system measures of performance connected with effectiveness in intelligence analysis?" To make progress on this question, we introduce a taxonomy of the functions AI systems could perform when supporting intelligence and analyze how errors in AI system output for each of these functions might propagate to produce consequences. In other words, we understand the effects of errors by the AI system by examining how those errors affect the process around the system depending on the role that the AI system serves (i.e., the function that it performs). For one function in our taxonomy, we create and analyze a mathematical model to demonstrate this process in detail. In addition to providing general insights about how existing metrics relate to AI system effectiveness, this model could be used to analyze the impact of AI systems in the field.

## Organization of This Report

### Scope

The scope of factors contributing to effectiveness considered in this report is narrow due to the limited resources available for this study. This report is concerned only with how the statistical performance of AI systems is connected to the impacts generated by the system. This performance is the property measured by standard performance metrics such as precision, recall and accuracy. There are categorically different properties of these systems that are likely germane to the contribution such systems make to mission success but are nonetheless outside the scope of this work. Perhaps the most straightforward example is the time it takes the system to return results in relation to the tempo of the mission supported.

More generally, the relationship among the human analysts using the system, the policymakers consuming the analysis, and the system itself is likely critical to successful use of the system. Is the output of the system and its level of certainty clearly communicated? Do human intelligence analysts feel that the system assists them or that it represents another chore to be completed? How does IC incorporate the results of quantitative analysis into intelligence products? What ethical concerns might attend to the particular use case envisioned? These questions, and others like them, are critical, and not addressed in this report.

Finally, this analysis implicitly takes place assuming a permissive environment for the AI system to operate in. That is, we do not consider how attacks on the underlying algorithm or on the infrastructure it needs to operate might affect analysis of the system's effectiveness. In the real world, such attacks are a realistic concern for IC and should be considered when assessing the risks that might flow from deploying an AI system. These risks could in principle be incorporated into the sort of model considered in this report, but further basic research into the susceptibility of AI systems to attack may be necessary to enable this.

## Research Approach, Audience, and Organization

In order to attack our central research question, we investigated three subsidiary questions:

1. How might AI be used to support the intelligence process, both as reflected in the development of real systems and in hypothetical systems that may not yet be in development?
2. How can we model the intelligence process for the purposes of determining how AI systems situated in this process affect it?
3. What metrics exist to characterize the performance of AI systems?

All three questions were addressed via the review of publicly available information, together with informal interviews of colleagues both inside and outside of RAND with backgrounds in AI and/or intelligence. For the first question, we relied on publicly available descriptions of AI projects supporting intelligence, such as those at the Joint Artificial Intelligence Center (JAIC) and Intelligence Advanced Research Projects Activity (IARPA). For the second question, we relied heavily on the intelligence literature, official national security, intelligence and defense doctrine publications, and works of scholar practitioners. For the third question, we utilized the extensive ML literature on performance measures, with a particular focus on binary classifiers due to the limited resources available for this study.

The primary audience for this report consists of decisionmakers within IC or DoD who may contemplate deploying an AI system to support intelligence missions. This report is intended to frame the problem of critically, rigorously, and quantitatively analyzing how much value these AI systems provide in steady-state operations and the extent to which they provide decisionmakers with the tools to strategize about how these systems might be best utilized to support their mission. We expect that a secondary audience of AI researchers, designers, and engineers building systems to support intelligence missions will likely also find this document useful for contextualizing the utility that their systems might provide to the intelligence process. In particular, we intend the primary and secondary audiences to use the contents of this report to "meet in the middle" and find a useful basis for communication about system requirements and capabilities. Finally, we suspect that the contents of this report might prove useful to a tertiary audience of AI system users and builders in noncommercial settings even outside of the context of intelligence. For example, we can envision many of these results being useful in the context of in-house cybersecurity efforts or even health care quality monitoring. Readers from contexts other than intelligence are encouraged to consider whether their processes and problems are analogous to those considered here.

## Key Terms

Here, we introduce a few terms that this report uses to convey specific concepts. In general, these are terms that are at risk of being understood colloquially, rather than in the narrow senses that serve the purposes of this report.

- **System versus model:** ML systems in particular are frequently referred to as "models" for the data used in their construction in technical circles. When discussing a mathematical model for the effectiveness of such a system, this usage can lead to unhelpful phrases such as "the model for model effectiveness" and render uses of the noun "model" ambiguous in certain contexts. To alleviate this issue, in this report we always refer to the system whose effectiveness we are trying to analyze as a "system" and the mathematical or qualitative model that assists us in this analysis as a "model." "System" always means system in this sense, and "model" always means model in this sense. However, do not exclusively use the word "system" to refer to a system of interest when a more specific term is available. For example, much of Chapter Three is devoted specifically to binary classifiers functioning as an ML system; in this case we refer to these systems as "binary classifiers" when speaking only about binary classifiers.
- **Deployment context/deploy:** The "deployment context" of a system refers to the things that system interacts with when in normal operation along with the configuration of those things and the manner of this interaction. For example, both a system's users and the way those users interact with the system are a part of the system's deployment context. Similarly, "deploying" a system refers to beginning to use the system to perform the task for which it was developed.
- **Performance versus effectiveness/impact:** Following a convention we did not originate, "performance" refers to how well a system completes a narrow definition of its task, while "effectiveness" or "impact" refers to whether the underlying goals of the system are achieved. For example, the performance of a computer vision system in a self-driving car concerns how often the system successfully recognizes a stop sign, and the effectiveness or impact concerns how often the car fails to stop at a stop sign.

- **Intelligence process:** This term refers to the process by which intelligence is collected, analyzed, and disseminated without invoking a particular model for this process. That is, the intelligence cycle is a conceptual model or framework for the intelligence process.
- **Metrics, or measures of performance/effectiveness:** By "metrics," or "measures of performance" or "measures of effectiveness," we mean numbers that capture properties of a system and bear on either the performance or effectiveness of that system.

## Artificial Intelligence and Machine Learning

"Artificial intelligence" refers to "computing technologies that exhibit what humans would consider to be intelligent behavior."[13] While this definition is intuitive, the judgment as to whether a task requires intelligence is somewhat subjective and depends on one's expectations of what computers can do. On a practical level, AI usually refers to the use of ML systems that utilize data to automatically learn the properties of a phenomenon of interest. ML has shown promise across a number of applications, from understanding the meaning of text and recognizing objects in images to building systems to automatically play competitive strategy games.[14] Other approaches to similar problems,

---

[13] National Academies of Sciences, Engineering, and Medicine, *Implications of Artificial Intelligence for Cybersecurity: Proceedings of a Workshop*, Washington, D.C.: The National Academies Press, 2019, p. 1-1.

[14] Alex Wang, Amanpreet Singh, Julian Michael, Felix Hill, Omer Levy, and Samuel R Bowman, "Glue: A Multi-Task Benchmark and Analysis Platform for Natural Language Understanding," Cornell University arXiv.org, February 22, 2019; Olga Russakovsky, Jia Deng, Hao Su, Jonathan Krause, Sanjeev Satheesh, Sean Ma, Zhiheng Huang, Andrej Karpathy, Aditya Khosla, Michael Bernstein et al., "ImageNet Large Scale Visual Recognition Challenge." *International Journal of Computer Vision*, Vol. 115, No. 3, 2015; David Silver, Aja Huang, Chris J. Maddison, Arthur Guez, Laurent Sifre, George van den Driessche, Julian Schrittwieser, Ioannis Antonoglou, Veda Panneershelvam, Marc Lanctot et al., "Mastering the Game of Go with Deep Neural Networks and Tree Search," *Nature*, Vol. 529, No. 7587, 2016.

typically called "rules-based" or "expert systems" approaches, make up the remainder of AI.[15]

ML itself is typically subdivided into three classes of techniques: supervised learning, unsupervised learning, and reinforcement learning.[16] Supervised learning is fundamentally concerned with prediction. Given a set of examples of some relationship such as images labeled by whether they contain a tank or text passages labeled by whether they pertain to chemical weapons, supervised learning techniques can be used to automatically construct a program predicting the presence of a tank in unlabeled images or identifying passages pertaining to chemical weapons in unlabeled text. Supervised learning is a close cousin to the classical statistical technique of regression—that is, finding the best fit line through a set of datapoints. The distinction between supervised learning and classical statistics is more cultural than technical in that classical statistics tends to be more concerned with using the system as a surrogate for understanding the phenomenon the system pertains to while supervised learning tends to be interested only in predictive power.[17]

Unsupervised learning techniques are designed to analyze data without a preidentified relationship of interest to extract some information about its structure. For example, Google's original architecture for its search engine utilized the PageRank algorithm, which determines which webpage is likely most relevant to a user's query and operates using unsupervised learning on the network of links in webpages.[18] Unsupervised learning can also be used to support supervised learning techniques within a given domain by learning statistical features in the data that can later be exploited for prediction. For example, the cur-

---

[15] National Academies of Sciences, Engineering, and Medicine, 2019.

[16] Jerome Friedman, Trevor Hastie, and Robert Tibshirani, "The Elements of Statistical Learning," *Springer Series in Statistics*, Vol. 1, No. 10, 2001; Richard S. Sutton and Andrew G. Barto, *Reinforcement Learning: An Introduction*, Cambridge, Mass.: MIT Press, 2018.

[17] Leo Breiman, "Statistical Modeling: The Two Cultures (with Comments and a Rejoinder by the Author)," *Statistical Science*, Vol. 16, No. 3, 2001.

[18] Friedman et al., 2001; Sergey Brin and Lawrence Page, "The Anatomy of a Large-Scale Hypertextual Web Search Engine," *Computer Networks and ISDN Systems*, 30.1-7, 1998.

rent dominant class of language analysis systems utilize unsupervised learning on massive amounts of unannotated language to learn general structures within the language of interest before a supervised learning step on a more limited dataset that reflects the statistical relationship of interest.[19] That is, unsupervised learning helps the system learn the overall statistical properties of text in general, giving it a head start on learning the statistical properties that predict the specific categories of interest. Returning to the example above about whether a text pertains to chemical weapons, one might first deploy these unsupervised techniques on a large volume of language data not annotated by whether it pertains to chemical weapons before proceeding to a supervised learning step with the annotated text. Unsupervised learning techniques can also be used to train generative models, which produce synthetic examples of a particular type of data (e.g., images), according to the statistical distribution of real examples. This is the technology underlying the production of "deepfakes," though this technology can also be used to build synthetic anonymized datasets to allow analysis while preserving privacy.[20]

Finally, reinforcement learning refers to a set of technique for automatically building systems to select actions according to uncertain rewards. These systems can be thought of as systems that learn to play a game successfully, either against the environment or against another player, by using the current state of the "board" to statistically select the most profitable next "move." Perhaps the most dramatic recent example of reinforcement learning at work is the success of AlphaGo, a system to play the game of Go.[21] Despite the massive space of actions available to choose from during each turn and the need for AlphaGo to optimize the long-term strategies that its short-term actions served,

---

[19] Jacob Devlin, Ming-Wei Chang, Kenton Lee, and Kristina Toutanova, "BERT: Pre-Training of Deep Bidirectional Transformers for Language Understanding," Cornell University arXiv, 2018.

[20] Yuezun Li and Siwei Lyu, "Exposing Deepfake Videos by Detecting Face Warping Artifacts," Cornell University arXiv, 2018; Yi Liu, Jialiang Peng, James J. Q Yu, and Yi Wu, "PPGAN: Privacy-Preserving Generative Adversarial Network," *2019 IEEE 25th International Conference on Parallel and Distributed Systems*, 2019.

[21] Silver et al., 2016.

AlphaGo was capable of beating a world-class human opponent, defeating Lee Sedol 4–1 in a five-game series.[22]

Across all three domains, ML systems learn from data through a process called "training." For each round of training, the ML system is evaluated on a subset of the data according to some measure of the system's quality. Typically, this measure is chosen for its mathematical properties rather than its practical value. The parameters in the ML system are then adjusted slightly to improve its performance on this data. From the perspective of this report, this represents an important philosophical point: ML systems are built through a process of optimization against some measure of performance, offering our first sign of the way these systems are shaped from start to finish by the way we choose to quantify their performance.

A full review of AI systems currently supporting intelligence analysis across IC or DoD is beyond the scope of this report. Nonetheless, we believe it is important to highlight select examples of AI systems to provide real-world context for our analysis.

Multidimensional Anomaly Detection fusing High Performance Computing, Analytics, and Tensors (MADHAT), an AI system out of JAIC, is an unsupervised learning system designed to assist analysts in detecting suspicious network traffic. Analysts are currently being trained to use the tool.[23] JAIC is developing another AI tool called "Entropy," which supports analysts concerned with the information environment, which might include information warfare analysts. The system assists human analysts with counter-information operations and psychological operations. Entropy currently identifies and summarizes real-time internet trends based on text and video.[24]

Project Maven is a prominent Pentagon AI effort that attempts to use ML to identify objects and people in full-motion video generated by unmanned aerial vehicles and thus supports analysts who evaluate

---

[22] Cade Metz, "In Two Moves, AlphaGo and Lee Sedol Redefined the Future," *Wired*, March 16, 2016.

[23] Joint Artificial Intelligence Center, "Joint Information Warfare," undated.

[24] Mark Pomerleau, "Pentagon's AI Center to Field New Psychological Operations Tool," C4ISRNET, September 11, 2020.

this footage for useful information and threats.[25] In recent public comments, the current JAIC chief technical officer (former acting JAIC director at the time), Nand Mulchandani, suggested that JAIC was working with Project Maven on "the algorithmic side but also on the deployment and testing side"; and Colonel Bradley Boyd stated that the JAIC's Smart Sensor project "is interacting with Maven as well as the Air Force on developing the Agile Condor pod capability to enable potentially autonomous sensing [and] autonomous tracking."[26] JAIC describes its Smart Sensor program as "a video processing AI prototype that rides on unmanned aerial vehicles and is trained to identify threats and immediately transmit the video of those threats back to manned computer stations for real-time analysis."[27]

The Palantir Gotham platform includes the Ava module, an AI tool used by analysts across DoD and IC. This module continuously looks for connections between data streams and integrated and federated data holdings, alerting human investigators of connections worth investigating. Palantir's Foundry, used by some government clients, allows users to build and deploy AI models themselves.[28]

---

[25] John Keller, "Project Maven Moves to ABMS to Showcase Technologies in Artificial Intelligence (AI) and Machine Learning," *Military & Aerospace Electronics*, September 8, 2020; Lizette Chapman, "Palantir Wins New Pentagon Deal with $111 Million from the Army," Bloomberg, December 13, 2019; Andrew Liptak, "Palmer Luckey's Company Earned a Contract for the Pentagon's Project Maven AI Program," *The Verge*, March 10, 2019; Frank Wolfe, "Testing Begins for Condor Pod to Enable AI-Powered MQ-9 Reaper Targeting," *Aviation Today*, September 14, 2020.

[26] Nand Mulchandani, Jane Pinelis, and Brad Boyd, "Joint Artificial Intelligence Center Leaders Update Reporters on DOD AI Developments," transcript, September 10, 2020. See also Src, Inc., "Teraflops of Processing Power at 26,000 Feet," 2018; Carlo Munoz, "JAIC Smart Sensor Plays Key Role in USAF Advanced ISR Pod Prototype," *Janes*, September 21, 2020; Joseph Trevithick, "MQ-9 Reaper Flies with AI Pod That Sifts Through Huge Sums of Data to Pick Out Targets," *The Drive*, September 4, 2020; Wolfe, 2020; Brandi Vincent, "How the Pentagon's JAIC Says It's Prioritizing Ethics in Its AI-Driven Pursuits," Nextgov, September 10, 2020; Nathan Strout, "Inside the Army's Futuristic Test of Its Battlefield Artificial Intelligence in the Desert," C4ISRNET, September 25, 2020.

[27] The Joint Artificial Intelligence Center, "The JCF and the Combatant Commands: A Symbiotic Relationship," *AI in Defense*, June 3, 2020.

[28] Palantir Technologies, Form S-1/A, 2020.

IARPA invests heavily in AI systems with utility to intelligence analysts, especially in its research areas of analysis, anticipatory intelligence, and collection. In the analysis space, IARPA has invested in programs such as Aladdin Video, Better Extraction from Text Towards Enhanced Retrieval (BETTER), Creation of Operationally Realistic 3D Environment (CORE3D), Deep Intermodal Video Analytics (DIVA), and Machine Translation for English Retrieval of Information in Any Language (MATERIAL). Aladdin Video developed technology to enable analysts to search massive numbers of video clips for specific events of interest with an eye toward analyzing the massive amounts of video uploaded to internet platforms.[29] BETTER funded performers for systems that extract and retrieve fine-grained semantic information, targeted for a particular analyst, from text, working across languages and domains to produce events structured as "who-did-what-to-whom-when-where," with an eye toward the massive amounts of unstructured text information being produced daily.[30] CORE3D funded performers that build systems that use satellite imagery, airborne imagery, and Geographic Information System (GIS) vector data to construct three-dimensional models of large geographic areas accurately, automatically, and quickly to improve situational awareness and support rapid military, intelligence, and humanitarian responses where manual methods for such modeling, while accurate, would be too time consuming.[31] DIVA funded performers who built systems that detected activities across multiple, ground-based camera streams with both overlapping and nonoverlapping viewpoints, with an eye toward assisting security professionals at airports, border crossings, or government facilities to analyze video streams from a large number of cameras.[32] Finally,

---

[29] IARPA, "Automated Low-Level Analysis and Description of Diverse Intelligence Video (ALADDIN) Broad Agency Announcement (BAA)," IARPA-BAA-10-01, June 28, 2010.

[30] IARPA, "Better Extraction from Text Towards Enhanced Retrieval (BETTER)," IARPA-BAA-18-05, September 28, 2018, p. 5.

[31] IARPA, "Creation of Operationally Realistic 3D Environment (CORE3D) Broad Agency Announcement," IARPA-BAA-16-06, November 1, 2016.

[32] IARPA, "Deep Intermodal Video Analytics (DIVA) Broad Agency Announcement," IARPA-BAA-16-13, March 17, 2017.

MATERIAL funded efforts to build an "English-in, English-out" information retrieval system that can take a domain-sensitive English query and return information retrieved from a multilingual repository as query-biased summaries in English.[33]

In the anticipatory intelligence space, IARPA has invested in programs such as Open Source Indicators (OSI), Cyber-Attack Automated Unconventional Sensor Environment (CAUSE), Hybrid Forecasting Competition (HFC), and Mercury. OSI funded performers who built systems that continuously analyze publicly available data to forecast major societal events, such as political crises, in an attempt to "beat the news."[34] Taking a similar approach with a cyber focus, CAUSE funded performers who built systems that attempted to provide warnings of cyberattacks with significant lead time, high recall, and low false discovery rate, based not only on conventional cyber information, but also on unconventional information sources such as social media.[35] Another similar program is Mercury, which focuses on using foreign SIGINT data to forecast events, such as terrorist activities, political crises, and disease outbreaks, with high accuracy and lead time.[36] Other projects, such as HFC, have sought to combine human forecasting and machine forecasting in hybrid approaches, with the machines compensating for the cognitive biases and lack of scalability of human analysis while the humans offer an ability to understand unusual or novel geopolitical issues.[37] In the collection space, IARPA has invested in programs such as Finding Engineering-Linked Indicators (FELIX) and Functional Genomic and Computational Assessment of Threats (Fun GCAT). FELIX funds performers that use AI to detect genetic engineering signatures. Determining that a given biological system is engineered allows the United States to rapidly respond to the accidental or delib-

---

[33] IARPA, "MATERIAL PD Announcement," August 1, 2016.

[34] IARPA, "Open Source Indicators (OSI)," IARPA-BAA-11-11, August 23, 2011, p. 3.

[35] IARPA, "Cyber-Attack Automated Unconventional Sensor Environment (CAUSE)," IARPA-BAA-15-06, July 17, 2015.

[36] IARPA, "Mercury Broad Agency Announcement," IARPA-BAA-15-08, June 12, 2015.

[37] IARPA, "Hybrid Forecasting Competition (HFC)," IARPA BAA-16-02, September 12, 2016; IARPA, "HFC Proposers Day Announcement," December 18, 2015.

erate release of engineered organisms that can pose health risks.[38] Fun GCAT funds systems that apply novel approaches to screening nucleic acid sequences and identifying sequences of concern to prevent the intentional or accidental creation of a biological threat.[39]

---

[38] IARPA, "Finding Engineering-Linked Indicators (FELIX) Broad Agency Announcement," IARPA-BAA-17-07, August 31, 2017.

[39] IARPA, "Functional Genomic and Computational Assessment of Threats (Fun GCAT) Broad Agency Announcement," IARPA-BAA-16-08, September 22, 2016.

# CHAPTER TWO

# Tracing Effectiveness from Mission to System

The output of an AI system is not an end unto itself. This means that the success of an AI system is defined by the success in achieving the objectives of the mission supported by the system utilizing the output of the system. In the context of intelligence, this manifests through the fact that no matter how self-contained any given AI system is, its output will contribute to informing intelligence assessments. These assessments give decisionmakers information about the world that they use to select courses of action that affect the security of the United States. The impact generated by the courses of action selected is the ultimate source of success or failure for the AI system. In a perfect world, the effectiveness of the system would be understood by tracing the effects backward along this chain of consequences. That is, the change in the security situation of the United States would be traced back to actions taken by the decisionmakers, which would be traced back to the intelligence used to select those actions, all the way back to the output of the system itself. In this way, the system would be judged by the net effect it had on the outcome we care most directly about: the overall security of the United States.

In a private-sector context, such a thorough analysis may even be possible, due to the limited scope of both the available actions and the definition of success. Ultimately the success of a company is determined by its financial situation. Particularly in a data-rich environment, the ease with which success that results from a financial definition of success can be measured may enable connecting system performance directly to this definition of success. For example, one could imagine a company such as Netflix connecting the performance of its recommender algorithm with data on user retention to construct a precise model of the revenue gained or lost by changes in the performance of the recommender algorithm.

Unfortunately, when analyzing such systems in the context of intelligence, effectiveness is not so obviously defined and measured. The value of intelligence cannot be reduced to dollars and cents. For example, a 2016 ODNI whitepaper, "Processes for Assessing the Efficacy and Value of Intelligence Programs," notes that "the efficacy of any particular program is difficult to assess" in part because individual programs "are not typically used in isolation."[1] This white paper then details the methodologies that ODNI utilized to assess the efficacy of collection programs in spite of this difficulty, at least at the time. Broadly speaking, these methodologies sought to capture how well the reporting generated conformed to priorities in the National Intelligence Priorities Framework (NIPF), how often these reports were cited in intelligence products, and how valuable the reports were perceived to be by intelligence professionals and consumers.

A comprehensive review of the problem of evaluating the effectiveness of the intelligence process or of present ODNI evaluation policy is well outside the scope of this report, and we do not intend to speak to the relative utility of this approach. However, it should be noted that the methodologies outlined in this white paper do not actually directly measure how effective the reporting emerging from a program is. To put a fine point on it: the procedure ODNI describes measures whether consumers are satisfied, not what impact the reporting generates. If, hypothetically, decisionmakers were faced with a choice between a program that generated reports that were frequently cited and satisfied intelligence consumers and a program that materially improved the security of the United States, they should choose the latter. These measures are therefore valuable primarily as a proxy for the positive effect on the security of the United States, which is more difficult to measure. Indeed, we need such proxies since actually tracing this effect back

---

[1]   ODNI, "Processes for Assessing the Efficacy and Value of Intelligence Programs," February 8, 2016, p. 1.

to the system is complicated and would require understanding how reporting influences analysts, how those analysts influence policymakers, and the concrete impacts of the actions selected by policymakers on the security and interests of the United States. This final step seems especially challenging, as it would require a deep enough understanding of the evolution of geopolitics to support analysis of how the state of the world would have changed if U.S. policymakers had chosen a different course of action.

One aspect of how ODNI addressed the challenge in the above example offers a hint as to a way forward in the context of analyzing the impact of AI systems. Implicitly, ODNI's approach measures efficacy by asking how well the reporting emanating from a program supports the next step (that is, analysis and the production of finished intelligence) along the chain from requirements through analysis to the action selected by the decisionmaker. To make this concrete, consider one of the measures of program efficacy used highlighted by ODNI in "Processes for Assessing the Efficacy and Value of Intelligence Programs": the number of times reporting from a program was cited in an intelligence product. This measure serves as a proxy for the effect of this program on the security of the United States by addressing the question of how well the program is supporting the next step in the chain, analysis, since citations are a direct measure of the utilization of reporting by analysts.

In this report, we organize our analysis of AI systems in a similar manner, judging AI systems by how well they support the next step in the intelligence process. Since we need a conceptual model for the process into which the AI system will be inserted in order to determine what the "next step" after the AI system is, we adopt the intelligence cycle as a model for the intelligence process. We define a set of four "system function categories" that are organized in part by the intelligence cycle and divide the functions of AI systems that support intelligence based on the properties of the "next step" they support. Put another way, these system function categories bin AI systems by how their output is utilized. The way the output is to be utilized provides a natural platform to analyze the consequences of errors in system output, which we can then trace back to understand how different error rates connect to different magnitudes of consequences at this "next step." For two of these categories (out of four in total), we find that this procedure yields ways of reasoning about the impact of such systems without grappling with the difficult questions of how intelligence and the actions selected by decisionmakers contribute to the overall security of the United States. For one of these two, we analyze a simple quantitative model of these consequences to demonstrate the power of this analysis. For the two other categories, we find that obstacles to this sort of detailed analysis of absolute efficacy remain, though workable baseline performance standards can be deduced.

A little additional context is called for before we launch into our analysis. First, we should note that strictly speaking these categories divide the functions that AI systems perform, not the systems themselves. So, entities that might have a single name and be thought of as a single system might nonetheless perform functions in multiple different categories. We will discuss this in more detail after the categories have been introduced. Second, we caution the reader against viewing the categories as too authoritative or definitive. They are intended as a useful conceptual framing device for this analysis and are almost certainly not the only way one could categorize AI systems supporting intelligence, in much the same way that there is no single definitive version of the intelligence cycle.

Additionally, the scope of the analysis enabled by this framework is limited by the fact that it considers only a single step downstream of the system. This means that it cannot be used to analyze whether the impact of a system is limited by a bottleneck farther downstream of the system whose deployment is being analyzed. For example, Lowenthal notes that processing and exploitation AI systems used in DoD's Project Maven or in the Defense Innovation Unit's Experimental xView Detection challenge seek to address the imbalance between data collected and the processing and exploitation of that data. However, as Lowenthal explains, sifting through all of the processed data and analyzing it take skills acquired through experience and training, which could be a bottleneck for a number of intelligence agencies.[2]

---

[2]  Lowenthal, 2020.

It will also become clear as we discuss examples that these categories abstract away details about the systems they are used to analyze. In particular, these categories are insensitive to the type of data on which the system operates, the engineering details of the system, and the mission and analysts that the system supports. This is by design, as at this level of abstraction one can separate important differences in the ways that the performance of systems in each category leads to impact without drowning in the wide variety of systems, missions, and analysts. However, in the section on "Information Prioritization" in Chapter Three, where we develop a quantitative model for the impact of systems in one of these categories, we will discuss the ways that adding back some of these details would enrich the analysis of a particular system. To the extent that this abstraction flows from using the intelligence cycle as a model for the intelligence process, we discuss how more detailed models of the intelligence process might support more detailed models of AI system effectiveness in the "Intelligence" section of this chapter.

The framework also cannot compare the deployment of an AI system to support one kind of analysis or stream of intelligence with investments to support another. That is, this framework cannot inform whether it is strategically more valuable to deploy an AI system to support the analysis of SIGINT or to spend those resources to hire additional foreign language or cultural experts. Since the ultimate goal of the framework is to support decisionmakers in analyzing the impacts of AI systems to support their development of organization strategy, these represent genuine limitations of our analysis, as well as opportunities for future research. However, since policymakers already have some tools for identifying limiting capabilities in their organization and weighing the benefits of disparate programs, this analysis should still prove useful even with those limitations. So, we merely emphasize that decisionmakers should be aware of these possibilities and include them in their analysis.

## On "Human Equivalent" Performance

For systems that replicate a task that is currently being performed by humans, one minimum standard of performance is always available to decisionmakers contemplating deploying an AI system: The performance of the system in question can be compared with that of the humans currently performing the task. For example, for a task where humans might reasonably be expected to disagree on some examples, such as assessing the objectivity of an intelligence product, the AI system to perform this task can be judged by whether it is at least as good at predicting the majority opinion as the average human performing the task. If this system is being considered for deployment to save time or effort on the part of the humans currently performing the task, this criterion is a reasonable baseline for system performance to demand before deployment. Though the exact risks might remain uncertain, the risks accepted by deploying the system are the same risks as in the existing process using humans to perform the task.[3]

While this approach is workable, it has important limitations even beyond the fact that it does not allow estimation of impacts aside from the resources needed to complete the task at a given level of risk. As will be discussed in Chapter Three, there are stronger and weaker ways to compare the performance of AI systems to determine which one is better. Roughly speaking, the strong definition of exceeding human performance requires the AI system to perform better regardless of which errors are more significant. However, depending on which errors are in fact more significant, AI systems might perform better than or equal to human performance in "impact-adjusted" terms, even though they are not better in the strong sense. Therefore, meeting or exceeding

---

[3]   Of course, this statement is true only within the scope of this report. That is, strictly speaking, only the risks due to the overall rate of errors while operating in a permissive environment are the same. The differing needs and vulnerabilities of computer systems and humans give rise to distinct risks. For example, replacing humans in a process with machines would likely increase the risk due to hacking but might decrease the risk due to pandemic disease. This also neglects any incidental benefits not given by the completion of the task itself, such as knowledge or information that is gained by the humans performing the task and that can then be leveraged to complete other tasks.

human performance is actually an especially strong criterion to enforce on the AI system.[4]

Furthermore, simply because the human and the machine make errors at the same rates does not mean they will make the same errors. For concreteness, consider a system that identifies vehicles in images. It is possible that the features of a given image that could cause humans to struggle with the task would be different from those that cause machines to struggle. Perhaps humans struggle to identify vehicles in images with poor lighting conditions while machines struggle with crowded images. If some class of images is particularly important, such as images with poor lighting conditions, then human equivalent performance needs to be defined in an even more fine-grained manner that differentiates between the performance on distinct classes of images.[5] Of course, in order to enable this fine-grained distinction, one needs a reproducible definition of the different classes of images of differing importance. These errors may also not be distributed identically in time. For example, if more than one human works with another to accomplish the task and these humans take shifts, error rates might differ between shifts, as we should expect some people to be more effective at the task than others.

The assumptions required to justify the analysis that the risk is equivalent before and after deployment are also more restrictive than they may first appear to be. Strictly speaking, the deployment of the AI system must be the only thing that changes. In particular, if the entire task is scaled up or down after deployment, the risks are not guaranteed to remain the same. For example, consider a hypothetical system

---

[4]  In terms of the concepts to be introduced in Chapter Three, the lack of a single summary metric for the performance of the system means that "better than human performance" needs to be interpreted as "better both in recall and specificity." Note that this also means we have no way of choosing a unique threshold for classification, since we have no criterion to use to choose among the whole range of thresholds that exceed human performance.

[5]  If the ratios of the importance of the different classes are known, then the overall performance can be re-weighted across these classes to take these ratios into account. However, if these ratios cannot be rigorously established, the only available criterion is the system exceeding human performance individually in each class, a yet more restrictive definition of exceeding human performance. It is the authors' judgment that this latter case should be expected to be typical.

that assesses the objectivity of intelligence products. Entirely for the sake of argument, suppose that if an intelligence product is assessed to be below some certain level of objectivity, this assessment has negative consequences for the analyst who authored the product, which they can appeal. Now, if the process by which products were reviewed were to transition from a team of humans reviewing a randomly sampled subset of intelligence products to an AI system reviewing all intelligence products, the total number of people receiving below-critical marks for objectivity despite being suitably objective will increase. This is because the greater number of products reviewed means that a fixed probability of false positives leads to a larger number of false positives. In addition to possibly being sensitive to the overall number of false positives for the sake of analysts who would otherwise have avoided the ordeal of an appeal, an increase in the resources of the office that handles appeals would be needed to match an increased volume. Failing to do so would result in an increase in the number of analysts facing negative consequences in error. Even if the capacity of this office does get increased, we should expect the number of analysts facing negative consequences in error to increase, since the appeals office likely makes errors as well.

## Intelligence

There is no standard definition of "intelligence" across defense and intelligence communities. For this study, we adopt the ODNI definition of intelligence as "information gathered within or outside the U.S. that involves threats to our nation, its people, property, or interests; development, proliferation, or use of weapons of mass destruction; and any other matter bearing on the U.S. national or homelands security."[6] There is also no standard definition of "intelligence analysis" across defense and intelligence communities. In this study, we settle on the definition provided by Rob Johnston in his landmark book, *Analytic Culture in the US Intelligence Community, An Ethnographic Study.*

---

[6] ODNI, "What Is Intelligence?" webpage, undated b.

Johnston defines intelligence analysis as the "socio-cognitive process, occurring with a secret domain, by which a collection of methods is used to reduce a complex issue to a set of simpler issues."[7]

### The Intelligence Cycle

The intelligence cycle is a conceptual model or framework for the intelligence processes. The intelligence process, as noted earlier, are those practical actions taken to collect, analyze, and disseminate information. Different interpretations exist in the defense and intelligence communities for how to exactly model the intelligence process. Disagreement can be found in the number and naming of steps that make up the intelligence cycle model. In this study, we refer to ODNI's intelligence cycle, which includes six steps: planning, collection, processing, analysis, dissemination, and evaluation.

1.  Planning involves determination of issues and needs that have to be addressed. These are formally called "intelligence priorities." These priorities inform how the intelligence is to be collected.
2.  Collection is the process of obtaining and assembling the data that will be analyzed. At this step, the data are often referred to as "raw intelligence," because they have not been analyzed and evaluated.
3.  Processing involves cleaning and synthesizing data into information so that intelligence analysts can make sense of it.
4.  Analysis is the examination, evaluation, and integration of information collected and the production of finished intelligence. Finished intelligence products are assessments of events, situations, and issues that include analytical judgments.
5.  Dissemination is the distribution of intelligence products or reports to decisionmakers, policymakers, and other intelligence analysts.

---

[7]  Rob Johnston, *Analytic Culture in the US Intelligence Community, An Ethnographic Study*, Washington, D.C.: CIA, Center for the Study of Intelligence, 2005, p. 37.

6.  Evaluation involves ensuring that intelligence products and reports, as well as the intelligence process, are relevant, free of bias, accurate, and timely. This step includes feedback from consumers.[8]

### Limitations of the Intelligence Cycle

The intelligence cycle is only a model of the intelligence process. That is, the lack of consistency in the number, naming, and understanding of steps in the model, actions, and activities performed at each step indicates that different organizations performing intelligence have different conceptual models for their process, despite all nominally having an intelligence mission. Whether or not these differences correspond to differences in the process at each of these organizations, this inconsistency is a signal that the intelligence cycle presented here is an imperfect reflection of the process of intelligence. Like all models, some details of the underlying phenomenon are lost in the process of abstraction. For instance, the intelligence cycle fails to distinguish among the six core intelligence collection disciplines of SIGINT, geospatial intelligence (GEOINT), HUMINT, IMINT, measurement and signature intelligence, and open-source intelligence.[9] The processes that produce each of these six types of intelligence might differ significantly, conceivably in ways germane to the effectiveness of an AI system supporting each of those processes.

For one example of a higher fidelity model of the intelligence process, consider Rob Johnston's analysis of the intelligence cycle model in which he identifies inputs, processes, and outputs to characterize the way information moves through the intelligence cycle in much the same way that a part moves through an assembly line.[10] This "systemic analysis" identifies points of friction between the intelligence cycle model and the reality of the intelligence process. For example, the intelligence cycle model does not account for repetitions of each step; it assumes the process is the same for every intelligence objective; and it

---

[8]  ODNI, "How the IC Works," webpage, undated a.

[9]  ODNI, undated b.

[10]  Johnston, 2005, chap. 4.

does not capture how each actor (human and/or machine) in the cycle contributes to the cycle itself or how the completion and activities of one step influence the start of the next step. Additionally, in reality the steps of the intelligence cycle model do not necessarily occur along the orderly single path that the cycle depicts. Depending on the situation, some steps are missed, and some bleed into others. This observation actually predates Johnston's work, going at least as far back as Gregory Treverton's "Real Intelligence Cycle," which depicts, for example, situations where analysis does not get published into a finished intelligence product, but rather leads directly to new intelligence requirements or times when collected raw data is so critical that it is immediately sent to a policymaker or decisionmaker (see Figure 2.1).[11]

In Johnston's case, the higher fidelity "process model" of the intelligence process is deployed to explore how the level of resources available to the analyst impacts the throughput of the process. The more careful analysis of how productivity depends on resources enabled by this process model, relative to that enabled by the standard intelligence cycle, suggests that improvements in assessing the utility of AI systems to intelligence analysis can be made by improving our model of

**Figure 2.1**
**Treverton's "Real" Intelligence Cycle**

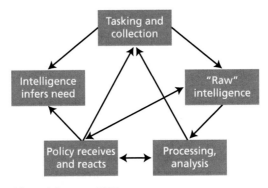

SOURCE: Adapted from Johnston, 2005.

---

[11] Johnston, 2005, p. 49.

how intelligence is analyzed. For example, models such as Johnston's may help identify "bottlenecks" farther upstream or downstream of the system and other similar effects. Such bottlenecks might be critical factors in determining the real value of a system assessed holistically, but would be missed using the methods outlined in this report.

Moreover, the intelligence cycle does not distinguish between the three common intelligence analysis levels known as "tactical," "operational," and "strategic" intelligence. Generally speaking, these intelligence analysis levels are distinguished from one another by the speed at which the intelligence analysis is performed to meet decisionmaker requirements, the consumers of the intelligence, and most important the scope of the analysis, with timescales, the seniority of the consumers, and the scope of the analysis generally increasing as the analysis moves from tactical toward strategic.[12] These levels are designed to aid intelligence analysts in understanding their responsibilities and decisionmakers in understanding the context and resources needed to provide analysis at a given level. From the perspective of this study, decisionmakers should anticipate that the ingredients for an effective AI system might differ among intelligence missions at different levels of analysis. Consequently, the way performance is measured and the standards set for AI system performance might depend on the level of analysis the system supports. For example, given the fact that strategic analysis occurs on longer timescales, analysts might have more time to review and corroborate the output of systems; this might lead to a greater tolerance for false positives. Understanding these levels can help decisionmakers develop strategies for where and how to deploy AI systems at each level and generalize about performance metrics and measures of effectiveness.

For this study, these gaps between the intelligence cycle and the actual practice of intelligence represent both a limitation and an opportunity for the future. As a limitation, these gaps raise the concern that our analysis will likely miss factors that drive the effectiveness of AI systems in much the same way that the intelligence cycle does not identify the burden placed on analysts. As an opportunity, however, John-

---

[12] ODNI, 2016.

ston's systemic analysis provides a roadmap for ways that future studies can begin to search for these effects in a systematic manner by analyzing the process in which both humans and machines operate.

## Artificial Intelligence System Function Categories

In this section, we introduce the four system function categories (see Figure 2.2 and Table 2.1) and qualitatively analyze the drivers of impact for AI systems that perform functions in each of these categories. We

**Figure 2.2**
**Relationship of the System Function Categories to the Intelligence Cycle**

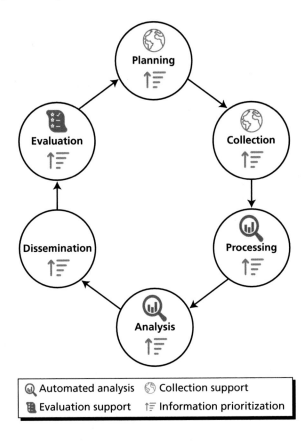

**Table 2.1**
**System Function Categories**

|  | Evaluation Support | Automated Analysis | Information Prioritization | Collection Support |
|---|---|---|---|---|
| Description | Ingests reports or products to determine their quality and their alignment with priorities | Transforms or enriches data without human supervision | Ingests available information and analyst preferences to connect analysts with useful information | Ingests available information to direct future collections |
| Example | A tool that classifies reports according to NIPF and tracks which priorities are being adequately collected on | A tool that transcribes, translates, and summarizes SIGINT | A recommender that flags reports for all source analysts based on previous interests or ratings | A system that uses SIGINT to direct IMINT to find or track a target |

NOTE: Examples are artificial/notional and do not necessarily reflect actual systems.

give examples of systems highlighted in the introduction that perform each of these functions and close with a discussion of systems that perform functions in multiple categories. To supplement observed real-world examples, we offer some hypothetical examples of systems. Both the real and hypothetical systems were chosen for the clarity with which they demonstrate the contours of the categories, and we do not intend to indicate that they are necessarily valuable or achievable systems. Over the course of this section and in the remainder of the report, we will speak of systems as falling into categories or being examples of a given category. This language facilitates discussion and is more intuitive. When faced with corner cases, however, the reader should keep in mind that this language really indicates that the system performs the function the category represents.

Ultimately, these categories are designed to enable analysis of the consequences of the errors of an AI system. They were therefore designed to separate the types of systems that give rise to distinct classes of consequences using the minimal number of categories. Historically, these categories emerged organically out of our discussions with subject-matter experts consulted for this effort. Starting with the intelligence cycle, however, one can obtain these systems by analyzing whether systems supporting a step in the intelligence cycle would produce qualitatively different consequences when making errors as opposed to those supporting a different step in the intelligence cycle. For those that do not produce such qualitative differences, if one collapses the categories, the three categories tied to the intelligence cycle will result. Alternatively, these categories could be thought of as reflecting a simplified three-step intelligence cycle of collection, analysis, and evaluation. These three categories should then be supplemented with the more general information prioritization category to capture a role for AI systems that we observed in development and in our interviews and that were not tied as closely to the step in the intelligence cycle being supported.

More broadly, though we refer to these categories as "AI" system function categories, by no means should a debate over whether a system truly represents AI preclude analysis in this framework. As we alluded to in Chapter One, questions of whether a system is truly an AI system can spark semantic debates. From the point of view of assessing impact, these debates are unhelpful. The ultimate guide should be whether the system performs functions that fall into the categories outlined in the following sections, since the criteria for these categories are designed to select for the necessary features to organize and enable analysis.

## Evaluation Support Systems

Evaluation support systems are those whose output is used in the evaluation step of the intelligence cycle. Put another way, these are systems whose output is used to monitor the intelligence process, determine how well it is functioning, and identify where it can be improved. For example, the 2016 ODNI whitepaper discussed briefly in the introduction to this chapter notes that "for reasons of feasibility and effectiveness, these methods [which count the citations of reports in intelligence products] focus on reports and citations that fit carefully defined criteria (e.g., based on topics of high interest)."[13] One could imagine using a computer system to assemble and analyze these counts at scale. If such

---

[13] ODNI, 2016, p. 3.

a system were to be built, it would be an evaluation support system. Similarly, one could imagine building a system to assist with or partially automate review of finished intelligence products, say by using natural language processing (NLP) to score each finished product for its objectivity, one of the five analytic standards in "Intelligence Community Directive 203: Analytic Standards."[14] Such a system would also be an evaluation support system.

Evaluation of current processes and effectiveness is a critical portion of the feedback loop through which IC makes improvements, reforms, and reinvestments. Therefore, errors in the output of an evaluation support system might affect choices about which programs to expand and which to cut, whom to promote and whom to lay off, and where the greatest value from new programs and innovations might lie. Unfortunately, these consequences are inexorably intertwined with the difficult question of understanding the overall effectiveness of the intelligence process. Thus, it does not appear that systems in this category can be analyzed for direct impact without grappling with that question in some form. When analyzing specific evaluation support systems, however, the details of the deployment context of that system might provide a means to rigorously identify and model impacts in a way that stops short of tracing the impact all the way to the actions selected by policymakers.

### Automated Analysis Systems

Automated analysis systems transform or enrich data without human supervision for the purposes of supporting intelligence analysis. Colloquially, we can think of an automated analysis system as being any system that draws conclusions about intelligence data. The critical feature of these systems is the fact that, while they use intelligence data to determine what they present to their users, they change them in some way rather than simply presenting the entirety of the data. For example, a system that crops out and presents only the most relevant piece of an image annotated with additional context would be an automated analysis system. These systems can support the processing, analysis,

---

[14] ODNI, "Intelligence Community Directive 203: Analytic Standards," 2015.

production, or dissemination steps of the intelligence cycle. For example, the system envisioned by IARPA's MATERIAL program would be an automated analysis system.[15] This program supports efforts to build "English-in, English-out" information retrieval, returning relevant documents in other languages along with English summaries of these documents that include the documents' relevance to the query. As output, the English summary might stand alone as capturing the contents of the document, especially when the user cannot read the language the document is written in.

As these systems are performing analytical work, the impacts they generate flow from the same place as those of any analytical work. If these systems make errors, we run the risk of misunderstanding the state of the world and selecting nonoptimal actions based on that misunderstanding. We will not belabor the difficulty in rigorously assessing this impact, as we have already touched on this point a number of times. However, this means that, as with evaluation support systems, we may not be able to rigorously assign impact without grappling with this issue.

If the system in question produces intelligence reports or finished intelligence products, we can sidestep this difficulty by evaluating these reports or products according to the same standards to which we hold human analysts. That is, we have already accepted that these standards will serve as our proxy for the impact of a report or product, so it is natural to evaluate the output of the machine in the same way. For these systems, the standards can function as the metrics of record for the system, provided they can be phrased in a sufficiently quantitative way. On the other hand, for systems that do not directly produce reports or products, we find ourselves in a situation identical to that discussed with regard to evaluation support systems.

## Information Prioritization Systems

Information prioritization systems help to direct the attention of a user, likely an intelligence analyst, to informational artifacts (e.g., reports, images, or intelligence products) in order to optimize the value of the

---

[15] IARPA, "MATERIAL PD Announcement," August 1, 2016.

information that the user can consume in a fixed amount of time. More concretely, we can imagine these systems as sitting between the user and a vast amount of information that cannot all be reviewed and helping the user choose which information should be reviewed first. These systems can assist at any point in the intelligence cycle, and indeed can be found even outside of the context of intelligence.[16] For example, within the context of intelligence, Palantir's AVA module (a part of its Gotham product) "alerts users to new . . . connections . . . ensuring that analysts spend time on their most important investigations," per a recent filing with the Securities Exchange Commission.[17] Though it is hard to parse precisely what the system does with the level of detail available, this description certainly suggests that this module performs an information prioritization role. As a general rule, warning systems, such as a cyber intrusion detection system, also perform an information prioritization role, since they serve to direct the attention of human users to the subject of the warning.

We will say much more about how to measure the effectiveness of an information prioritization system in the next chapter. However, even without descending into the mathematical details, one can see that these systems enable more detailed analysis of the implications of their performance than the two categories discussed above. These systems ultimately serve to allocate a resource, the subset of analyst time devoted to their use. Their effectiveness is then determined by whether they allocate that resource prudently or wastefully. The outcome of the allocation directed by the system, what proportion of the useful items is actually identified by the analyst using the system, is the return on the investment of analyst time directed by the system. As a practical matter, some approximation of this return must be available as a side effect of system construction, since in order to train a system to iden-

---

[16] For an example in the context of health care quality monitoring, see Daniel Ish, Andrew M. Parker, Osonde A. Osoba, Marc N. Elliot, Mark Schlesinger, Ron D. Hays, Rachel Grob, Dale Shaller, and Steven C. Martino, *Using Natural Language Processing to Code Patient Experience Narratives: Capabilities and Challenges*, Santa Monica, Calif.: RAND Corporation, RR-A628-1, 2020.

[17] Palantir Technologies, Form S-1/A, 2020.

tify which items will be useful for an analyst to look at, the designers must have a definition of utility that is consistent and measurable.

Though this analysis enables the construction of a consistent definition of the effectiveness of an information prioritization system, it is important to remember that this is ultimately a proxy for the true effectiveness of the system. While the resources spent by the system (both analyst time and the financial resources needed to assemble and maintain the system) are clearly and unambiguously measurable, the definition of utility of an item for the analyst, which serves as the return on the investment for the AI systems investment of these resources, is almost certainly ultimately given by some proxy. That is, chances are that the system is built not by predicting the ultimate impact on the security of the United States of an individual item to be recommended, but by predicting some more accessible quantity such as the utility that the analyst perceives the item to have.

## Collection Support Systems

Collection support systems are those whose output serves to direct or trigger the collection of new intelligence. Put another way, these are systems whose output has a hand in the question of where a camera gets pointed, where an Intelligence, Surveillance, and Reconnaissance drone flies, or which new lead is forwarded on to a case officer. Collection support systems therefore necessarily support functions in the planning and direction or collection steps of the intelligence cycle.

At the most basic level of analysis, collection support systems have a lot in common with information prioritization systems. A sensor cannot be pointed everywhere at once, so these systems choose what it does and does not point at. If the sensor fails to develop useful information, the sensor time was wasted in much the way an error from an information prioritization system wastes user time. Similarly, the return on the investment of "sensor time" is set by the reporting that emanates from the program directed in part by the collection support system. So, much of what will be discussed in Chapter Three will apply at least to some extent to these systems.

The collection support and information prioritization categories quickly distinguish themselves when one considers what models with a greater level of detail might look like. As addressed in more depth in the next chapter, for information prioritization systems more detail can be added by modifying the process by which the reports arrive to the information prioritization system and are forwarded in order to account for the differences in tempo between recommendation and warning systems, whereas in the case of collection support systems, one could imagine including any role these systems might have in managing the platforms for collection, weighing both the efficiency with which these systems allocate resources and any risk to the integrity of the platforms themselves. Building a more detailed model of the deployment context of a collection support system may also, depending on the system, benefit from utilizing the literature on tracking theory.[18]

## Systems Spanning Multiple Categories

We have already mentioned that AI systems can fall into multiple categories in this framework. To illustrate this phenomenon, consider the hypothetical analyst's AI-powered digital assistant discussed by Josef Gartin in "The Future of Analysis." Gartin imagines this assistant briefing an analyst in the morning on the state of the government of "Farlandia," which the analyst had previously predicted was at risk of political instability. This morning, the assistant tells her, among other things, that "the global base rate for a no-confidence vote in similar situations over the past 40 years is 67 percent" (indicating automated analysis functionality); that "there is new, sensitive compartmented reporting relevant to your account" (indicating information prioritization functionality); and that "your personal accuracy rating has fallen three points to 47 percent" (indicating evaluation support functionality).[19] While we do not have any direct evidence of this hypothetical system helping to manage collection, it seems in the spirit of Gartin's discussion to imagine the system taking general questions such as "Where is the finance minister of Farlandia today?" and con-

---

[18] See, e.g., Y. Bar Shalom, and X. R. Li, *Multisensor, Multitarget Tracking: Principles and Techniques*, Storrs, Conn.: YBS, 1979.

[19] Gartin, 2019, p. 4.

verting them into tasking. With this supposition, this single system performs functions in all four of our categories.

This hypothetical system actually serves as an excellent example of the ways in which the categories, rather than breaking down when more than one category is at work, help to organize and enable analysis. If we were faced with Gartin's hypothetical analyst's digital assistant and asked to evaluate how well it was performing, we might find ourselves disoriented by the sheer number of things the assistant does and the unstructured natural language form of its output. Walking through the system categories allows us to separate out distinct functions by thinking about how the analyst uses each piece of the output.

For a real-world example, consider IARPA's CAUSE, which funded research into systems to forecast and detect cyberattacks at their earlier phases, such as reconnaissance and planning, and to detect and counter adversary campaigns before they reach more damaging phases.[20] Since the system this program envisions issues warnings that direct the attention of a cyber-analyst, it is an information prioritization system. However, since these warnings do not consist solely of the underlying data the system used to make the determination, but rather also include a prediction of when and how the attack will occur, it is also an automated analysis system.

---

[20] IARPA, "Cyber-Attack Automated Unconventional Sensor Environment (CAUSE)," webpage, July 17, 2015.

# CHAPTER THREE

# Measuring Performance and Effectiveness

In this chapter, we offer a self-contained treatment of the problem of rigorously measuring the performance and effectiveness of an AI system. For the most part, the discussion is confined to binary classifiers, which make a simple yes-or-no decision about data, and to information prioritization systems. Even with the discussion limited in this way, general lessons can be learned and are likely portable to other types of AI systems. Though this chapter touches on rather technical subjects, every effort has been made to keep it accessible to a general audience. Consequently, many of the technical details have been removed to a supporting appendix. Ultimately, the topics discussed in this chapter are inexorably intertwined with the problem of analyzing the properties and performance of an AI system to understand what value such a system might provide to an organization and how to best utilize such a system. We intend the concepts introduced here to provide a useful set of conceptual tools to enable decisionmakers to be critical consumers of these systems, even though they may never build one themselves.

## Metrics, Measurement, and Communication

In the dominant methodology for characterizing the performance of AI systems, the only attribute of interest is its likely performance on unseen data, characterized statistically.[1] To estimate this likely perfor-

---

[1] Though this methodology is typically couched in contrast with classical statistical techniques for model evaluation, one can adopt the same methodology when evaluating the per-

mance, we proceed as if we are experimenting on an AI system that dropped out of the sky. We begin by selecting a set of metrics to represent the performance of the AI system. Possible metrics include the myriad of metrics for binary classifiers discussed in the next subsection, similar quantities for other problem domains, and properties such as the time it takes the system to return an answer.

Then, we assemble a set of data, the test data, that is representative of the data the system will encounter during deployment, and the metrics are measured on that dataset in order to estimate the true value of these metrics.[2] For example, the time it takes the system to process each datapoint in the test data might be recorded, and the average of those processing times used as an estimate of the average time the system is expected to spend processing any given datapoint once it is deployed. For ML systems in particular, it is also important to ensure that the test data do not reuse any data from the training process, as such systems should be expected to do better on those data than on data not used in training.[3]

Within this methodology, these quantifiable properties serve as a surrogate for the system itself in much the same way that the measured ability of a vehicle to accelerate under load might be used to stand in for the vehicle when considering its ability to tow a load. Were one to procure a vehicle for the purpose of towing, one would communicate about the requirements of this vehicle by specifying the load that the vehicle needs to be able to accommodate. Analogously, if one was to procure an AI system to fill some role in an organization, choosing a set of metrics and specifying the needed performance in terms of these metrics would *define the requirements for the AI system.* In the course of the design process, engineers will attempt to optimize the system with respect to the metrics provided. We will see in the next section

---

formance of any system designed to solve a given problem, regardless of whether that system was built using machine learning. See Breiman, 2001.

[2]   The situation is somewhat more complicated in the case of reinforcement learning, as there the system takes actions and receives rewards rather than simply processing data from a fixed distribution. Ultimately the mode of evaluation still proceeds by experimentation in much the same manner, however. See, e.g., Silver et al., 2016.

[3]   Friedman, 2001.

that different choices of metrics can disagree as to which system is performing better, meaning that different choices of metrics reflect different priorities for the system and result in different design choices on the part of engineers attempting to construct the best system. If metrics are mis-specified or left ambiguous when communicated to AI system engineers, then the system requirements that these metrics represent are mis-specified or left ambiguous, which, in turn, results in a system that may not meet users' needs or reflect their priorities. In addition to enabling post hoc reasoning about the properties of a fixed system, therefore, specifying metrics of record for a system is the central means of communicating the properties required of this system to those building it. Defining the metrics that will be used to measure performance is the most concrete way for system users to communicate their needs and priorities to system designers.

If we use measurement of our desired metrics on the test dataset to reason about the properties of the system in deployment, we must understand any general limitations of this experimental design and be able to connect those with possible risks. For example, ultimately this process relies on the data available to test the system being representative of the data the system will encounter after deployment. This could flatly fail to be true when the dataset is assembled, if representative data are unavailable or if some detail of how the data were collected skews their distribution relative to that of the data the system will encounter after deployment. For example, when testing a system that identifies tanks in images, perhaps there are no available images of one particular model of tank fielded by an adversary when the system is being tested. Moreover, even if the data were representative at the time they were assembled, the underlying phenomenon might shift over time. Continuing with the above example, perhaps after the system has already been deployed, an adversary fields an entirely new model of tank.

To give a real-world example, privacy issues have generally complicated the task of assembling a representative set of test data for spam filters.[4] Since spam filters distinguish legitimate emails from spam, a

---

[4]  Vangelis Metsis, Ion Androutsopoulos, and Georgios Paliouras, "Spam Filtering with Naive Bayes—Which Naive Bayes?" *CEAS*, Vol. 17, 2006.

test set needs legitimate emails on which to test the performance of the filter whose sender and recipient might consider private and be unwilling to share. A dataset could be assembled of publicly shared emails, like those sent to public mailing lists, but these might not be representative of the emails between individuals, because public emails may exclude topics and data considered personal or of a private nature. Similarly, relying on voluntarily shared emails risks the possibility that the very characteristics of the message or participants that lead to the sharing of the message restricts the degree to which a dataset assembled in that way represents all email. For example, this, too, might lead to a dearth of emails about personal topics relative to a truly random sample of all extant emails. One of the larger public email datasets is actually composed of emails from the work accounts of Enron employees, which were made public as a consequence of the fraud investigation.[5] While this circumvents the issue of whether voluntary sharing might render a dataset of emails unrepresentative, it is not immediately obvious whether restricting the dataset to emails from and to a single company, in a single sector, in a single location, that was engaged in a massive fraud might also introduce idiosyncrasies into the dataset.

Additionally, there is an important distinction between the *sample* value of a metric and the *actual* value of that metric. The sample value is calculated using the test data, while the actual value is the value one would obtain with an infinite amount of test data. The smaller the sets of data, the more the value of the metric should be expected to vary between different sets of data. Returning to the above example of a system that identifies tanks in images, if we tested such a system on a test set containing 100 images, it might return 72 images correctly (i.e., correctly label them as possessing or not possessing a tank). This would lead us to conclude that the system has a sample accuracy of 72 percent. Were we to assemble a much, much larger test set containing millions of images, we might find that the system has an accuracy of 67.5 percent. This would indicate that the system made a "lucky guess" with about five images on the initial, smaller test set.

---

[5]   Metsis et al., 2006.

Classical statistics has a number of techniques to quantify this variation, but a thorough inventory is well outside the scope of this report.[6] A consumer of these estimates of metrics of performance need only confirm that some quantification was attempted, or that "error bars" are given, denoting the likely extent of the variation. Such a consumer should also confirm that the anticipated variation does not extend over a range that renders the value of the system ambiguous. In the context of the above example, these error bars might indicate a 95-percent probability that the true accuracy lies between 62.5 percent and 80 percent. Also, as a practical matter, note that as the amount of data increases, the anticipated range of variation should decrease to match the expected variation in the sample quantity. However, simply increasing the amount of test data cannot address whether the test data are representative of the data that will be encountered in deployment, however.

Consumers of these metrics should also look out for "multiple testing" issues. The classical statistical techniques used to create the error bars can bound only the probability that the actual value of a metric lies outside of the error bars. When multiple quantities are of interest, the small chance that any given quantity lies outside of its error bars can translate to a significant risk that at least one lies outside of its error bars. Essentially, rare things become more common when there are multiple opportunities for them to happen. Elaborating on the running example of an image analysis system that detects tanks, we might consider a system that detects and identifies ten different types of tanks. Without mitigation, a 95-percent chance that the accuracy of the system on any given type of tank lies within the specified error bars translates to as much as a 40-percent chance that the accuracy on at least one type of tank lies outside, possibly below, the given range. There are well-established techniques for mitigating these issues, but system acquirers may want to confirm that one of these techniques has in fact been deployed and anticipate the fact that they will generally result in wider error bars.

---

[6]   For a thorough discussion, see, e.g., George Casella and Roger L. Berger, *Statistical Inference*, Vol. 2, Pacific Grove, Calif.: Duxbury, 2002.

Finally, since training a system necessarily changes its performance, systems that continue training after deployment, as in recommenders that adapt based on their interactions with users, are more challenging to evaluate than systems that follow a simple three-step procedure of train, test, deploy. One option to mitigate this is testing the system after each new round of training, forming a cycle of the three steps in the simple procedure. While this is feasible, it could become statistically complicated due to the multiple testing issue described above. To address this, one might be drawn to the idea of testing periodically to detect how much improvement the system has accrued through training and assuming between tests that the system must be performing at least as well as its last test. Unfortunately, the phenomenon of double descent, wherein system performance improves, then degrades, then improves again as training proceeds for certain classes of systems, indicates that this assumption is not universally true.[7] Understanding these sorts of deployments would be aided by a theoretical understanding of how system performance scales with training and data availability. To our knowledge, no general theoretical results about this subject exist, though recent progress has been made in the context of systems for analyzing text in particular.[8]

**Metrics for Binary Classifiers**

As noted in the previous subsection, metrics are the central means of communication between system designers and users, and ML systems in particular are designed to maximize the precise objective for which they are designed. These relationships set up a feedback loop between metric choice, risk preferences, and system design. Consequently, a detailed understanding of metrics for the evaluation of these systems is advisable for system users and acquirers. As we will see, even when characterizing the performance of these simple systems, one encoun-

---

[7]   Preetum Nakkiran, Gal Kaplun, Yamini Bansal, Tristan Yang, Boaz Barak, and Ilya Sutskever, "Deep Double Descent: Where Bigger Models and More Data Hurt," Cornell University arXiv, 2019.

[8]   Jared Kaplan, Sam McCandlish, Tom Henighan, Tom B. Brown, Benjamin Chess, Rewon Child, Scott Gray, Alec Radford, Jeffrey Wu, and Dario Amodei, "Scaling Laws for Neural Language Models," Cornell University arXiv, 2020.

ters a wide array of metrics without a clear "best" choice for all circumstances. Indeed, though this subsection covers a large number of evaluation schemes, we do not have the space to exhaustively discuss all existing metrics even for this simple type of system.

By "binary classifier," we mean a system that makes a simple yes-or-no determination about each datapoint. The prototypical example is a spam filter, which ingests an email and determines whether it is likely to be unsolicited and unwanted (spam), or a legitimate email of interest to the user (not spam). Given the perennial problem of unwanted email, it is perhaps unsurprising that a number of approaches to creating such a system has been explored, spanning both the rules-based and statistical approaches.[9]

In more detail, we will call the two conditions the system seeks to choose between "positive" and "negative." In the example of a spam filter, we could assign spam as positive (the presence of the condition of interest) and not spam as negative (the absence of that condition). When comparing the labels assigned by the classifier to the true labels, there are four possible outcomes on each datapoint: true positive (tp), true negative (tn), false positive (fp), and false negative (fn). A true positive is an example (an email) that does in fact possess the condition of interest (is spam, positive) and was correctly labeled as possessing the condition by the system (marked as spam by the filter, labeled positive). A false positive, on the other hand, is an example that does not possess the condition of interest (is not spam, negative) but is nonetheless labeled as possessing the condition by the system (marked as spam by the filter, labeled positive). True negative and false negative are identical with all conditions reversed, respectively.

Since these four cases are the only possible outcomes of a classification decision by the classifier, the rate at which each happens is sufficient to capture the performance of the classifier. However, only two of these quantities are actually necessary to characterize the performance of the classifier itself, since rates at which the four cases happen must

---

9   Mithilesh Kumar Paswan, P. Shanthi Bala, and G. Aghila, "Spam Filtering: Comparative Analysis of Filtering Techniques," *IEEE-International Conference on Advances in Engineering, Science and Management (ICAESM-2012)*, 2012.

satisfy two constraints independently of how the classifier is performing: a fixed total number of datapoints and a fixed number of datapoints that are actually positive regardless of their label. Unfortunately, the two degrees of freedom (i.e., two quantities) left after satisfying those two constraints are independent properties of the classifier and so must both be specified to fully capture the classifier performance. Strictly speaking, a wide variety of pairs of metrics could be used to capture these two independent properties, provided that the members of the pair are suitably independent from one another.[10] In practice, when intending to completely specify classifier performance in this way, any two of the four metrics in Table 3.1 are typically chosen. In the authors' experience, recall and specificity or recall and precision appear to be the most common pairs.

The entries in Table 3.1 illustrate one way of understanding the necessity of using two numbers to fully capture classifier performance: Performance on positive examples can vary entirely independently from performance on negative examples. Take, for example, recall and specificity. Recall captures information about how well the classifier is doing on positive examples, and specificity captures information about how well the classifier is doing on negative examples. A classifier with high recall does not make many false negative errors, while a classifier with high specificity does not make many false positive errors. Classifiers with a high recall and a low specificity successfully identify most of the positive examples in the data but mark many negative examples as positive alongside them. Roughly, one can think of this as resulting in a group of data that is labeled positive and contains the majority of the positive examples along with a significant number of false positives and a group of data labeled negative largely depleted of positive examples.[11]

Of course, needing to specify two numbers to completely capture classifier performance means that for some pairs of classifiers there is no obvious "best" classifier. If classifier A has both a higher recall and higher specificity than classifier B, classifier A is strictly better than classifier B. If, however, classifier A has a higher recall but lower speci-

---

[10] For more detail on this subject, see the appendix.

[11] Exactly how true this picture is depends on the overall prevalence of positive datapoints.

**Table 3.1**
**Basic Binary Classifier Measures of Performance**

| Formula | Names | Complement Name | Description |
|---|---|---|---|
| $\dfrac{tp}{tp+fn}$ | **Recall**, true positive rate | False negative rate | Recall is the proportion of the positives that are labeled positive (e.g., the percentage of the images that contain a tank that are labeled as containing a tank). |
| $\dfrac{tn}{tn+fp}$ | **Specificity**, true negative rate | False positive rate | Specificity is the proportion of negatives that are labeled negative (e.g., the percentage of the images that do not contain a tank that are labeled as not containing a tank). |
| $\dfrac{tp}{tp+fp}$ | **Precision**, positive predictive value | | Precision is the proportion of examples labeled positive that are actually positive (e.g., the percentage of the images labeled as possessing a tank that possess a tank). |
| $\dfrac{tn}{tn+fn}$ | **Negative predictive value** | | The negative predictive value is the proportion examples labeled negative that are actually negative (e.g., the percentage of the images labeled as not possessing a tank that do not possess a tank). |

SOURCES: Tom Fawcett, "An Introduction to ROC Analysis," *Pattern Recognition Letters*, Vol. 27, No. 8, 2006; Douglas G. Altman and J. Martin Bland, "Statistics Notes: Diagnostic Tests 2: Predictive Values," *BMJ*, Vol. 309, No. 6947, 1994.

NOTE: *tp* stands for the probability that the labeled example will be a true positive, *fp* the probability of a false positive, *tn* the probability of a true negative, and *fn* the probability of a false positive. The complement name is the name given to one minus the quantity given, when that is used in place of the quantity itself. The names given in this table are not exhaustive of those used in the literature but capture the authors' judgment as to the most essential names.

ficity than classifier B, whether classifier A is better than classifier B depends on whether false negatives or false positives represent a bigger problem. In order to adjudicate situations like this, we can specify a single metric that combines the two independent degrees of freedom for classifier performance. For example, precision and recall are sometimes combined into the $F_1$ score[12] to give a single number that cap-

---

[12] Peter A. Flach, "The Geometry of ROC Space: Understanding Machine Learning Metrics through ROC Isometrics," *Proceedings of the 20th International Conference on Machine Learning (ICML-03)*, Washington, D.C., 2003.

tures some information about performance on positive and negative examples simultaneously. In symbols,

$$F_1 = \frac{2 \times precision \times recall}{precision + recall}.$$

Choosing a single metric to represent classifier performance in this way allows unambiguous comparison of any pair of systems. Measured by $F_1$, classifier A is performing either better than, worse than, or equivalently to classifier B. The converse is also true: Any way of unambiguously ranking pairs of systems is equivalent to choosing a single metric to capture system performance.[13] Since choosing this metric corresponds to adjudicating the ambiguous cases when which system is better depends on whether false positives or false negatives are more detrimental, metric choice is an implicit statement of risk preference between false positives and false negatives.

For many of the traditional metrics used to characterize the performance of binary classifiers, this statement of risk preference remains implicit due to the lack of a clear line between the way the metric measures performance and the effect the system has on its surroundings. For example, the impact of a marginal increase in $F_1$ on the effectiveness of system is unclear. In the absence of an argument for why $F_1$ is directly related to the effectiveness of the system, the implicit risk preference declared by $F_1$ cannot be connected to concrete risks in the real world. While this issue is present for many extant metrics, one class of metrics, which will be introduced in the next section, is designed specifically to connect the metric constructed to the actual effectiveness of the system under consideration.

### Accuracy and Cost Models

Perhaps the most immediately recognizable metric for binary classifier performance is *accuracy*, the proportion of the examples labeled by

---

[13] This result is subject to some mild assumptions about the continuity of the ranking system. See the appendix for more detail.

the model that it gets right. That is, accuracy of the proportion of true positives and true negatives among all datapoints. In symbols,

$$accuracy = tp + tn.$$

Among the metrics discussed so far, the implicit values expressed by the use of accuracy are unusually clear: Accuracy treats the value of the two types of errors as precisely equal regardless of the overall error rate. That is, if we envision a hypothetical system that performs some task which results in a $1 reward for a correct classification and no reward or penalty for incorrect classifications, the expected reward is $1 times the accuracy. Similarly, if there is a $1 penalty for each incorrect classification and no reward for a correct classification, the expected penalty is proportional to one minus the accuracy.

This ease of interpretation also offers an especially sharp demonstration of how metric choice can fail to match the actual value provided by the classifier. If the costs of the two types of errors are not actually equal, accuracy gives a false impression of the effectiveness of the classifier. For example, in the case of a tactical missile warning system, false negative errors are likely to be considerably more costly than false positive errors. In many practical situations, this mismatch between accuracy and the actual effectiveness of the system is exacerbated by the tendency of the more important class to be the rarer one. That is, though missile attacks are more important to successfully spot than the lack thereof, the base is likely to spend most of its time not under attack. In such cases, the accuracy might be misleadingly inflated by the sheer number of times the system correctly does not raise the alarm, possibly concealing poorer performance on the more important case.

Metrics that are broadly similar to accuracy but that account for the possibility of some cases being more critical than others can be constructed through a technique called "cost-sensitive classification."[14] In cost-sensitive classification, one assigns a value to each of the four

---

[14] Charles Elkan, "The Foundations of Cost-Sensitive Learning," *Proceedings of the 17th International Joint Conference on Artificial Intelligence*, Vol. 2, August 2001.

possible classification outcomes and asks what the average value of the classifier's decisions are. The best classifier is then the one that has the highest average value, taking into account the impact of the classification decisions. In symbols, this corresponds to using the metric

$$cost = (benefit\ of\ a\ true\ positive) \times (percentage\ of\ true\ positives)$$
$$+ (cost\ of\ a\ false\ positive) \times (percentage\ of\ false\ positives)$$
$$+ (benefit\ of\ a\ true\ negative) \times (percentage\ of\ true\ negatives)$$
$$+ (cost\ of\ a\ false\ negative) \times (percentage\ of\ false\ negatives).$$

This can be regarded as a straightforward generalization of accuracy, since accuracy is simply the expected cost if *benefit of a true positive* = *benefit of a true negative* = 1 and *cost of a false positive* = *cost of a false negative* = 0.

Balanced accuracy, another common metric for classifier performance, is measured by the value of correctly identify rare phenomena: The rarer a phenomenon is, the more valuable correctly identifying it is. Balanced accuracy can be phrased as a cost model with

$$benefit\ of\ a\ true\ positive = \frac{1}{percentage\ of\ positives},$$

$$benefit\ of\ a\ true\ negative = \frac{1}{1 - percentage\ of\ positives}.$$

That is, balanced accuracy values positive examples inversely proportional to how common they are.

Cost models can be a powerful way of measuring the practical effectiveness of a classifier, provided there is a way of assigning the relevant costs. When the classifier is deployed in a private-sector context, cost models may be quite straightforward to apply, since costs and benefits to the model's operation can be expected to be dollar-denominated and relatively easy to determine. For example, if the classifier in question is designed to guide the placement of ads in front of the individuals most likely to respond to those advertisements by purchasing the product in question, the cost of a false positive is simply the cost of the ad while the benefit to a true positive is the profit from the sale less the cost of the ad. Similarly, the cost of a false negative and the benefit of a true negative are zero since no ad is placed and no sale is made. The metric constructed from these values is the expected profit from using this system (neglecting the costs of deploying and maintaining the system and those of the alternative), which is precisely the value provided by the classification decisions of the system.

In the context of intelligence, however, cost models are likely to be significantly less applicable. In addition to the general difficulties in rigorously assigning a number to the benefits provided by intelligence, as discussed in Chapter Two, intelligence applications are unlikely to present costs and benefits that can simply be added together. Returning to the missile warning system, the resources spent by a false positive, the normal operations disrupted by the preparations for an attack that will not come, cannot be directly compared with the consequences of a false negative, the lives and equipment lost in an attack for which the base was unprepared. That is, these two sets of consequences are not even in the same units, much less of the same magnitude.

### Erring on the Side of Positives Versus on the Side of Negatives

As discussed in the previous sections, the use of a single metric constitutes a decision about the relative value of positive and negative examples. This decision, as with all decisions about how to value performance, feeds back into the design of the AI system itself. In addition to the broader feedback effect that this has on shaping the engineering of the system through the requirements and metrics of record chosen, there is a narrow way that metric choice drives choices of system parameters: through the decision of whether the system should, broadly speaking, err on the side of false positives or false negatives.

In general, binary classifiers can be adjusted to be either more reticent or more willing to mark an example as positive, depending on the preferences of the system designer. The mechanism for this design freedom is perhaps easiest to grasp in the case of *score*-based classifiers.[15] These classifiers do not produce a classification decision directly; instead, they produce a number, called a "score," that represents the

---

[15] Flach, 2003.

classifier's level of belief that an example possesses the quality of interest. For example, a score-based spam filter might mark an email that shows all the hallmarks of a poorly constructed phishing scheme with a 0.99, indicating that this email is very suspicious, while assigning only a 0.55 to a sophisticated spear-phishing email, thereby indicating only that there is something a little off about it. This score is then compared with a *threshold* in order to turn it into a hard yes-or-no classification. In this example, perhaps the engineers have set the threshold at 0.5, meaning both of these emails would be marked as spam.

The choice of threshold is a "knob" that can be turned in order to control whether the classifier errs on the side of classifying an example as positive or negative.[16] Analogizing the classifier to an alarm system, we can imagine this "knob" as controlling how readily the classifier raises the alarm,—for example, whether the perimeter detection system on an embassy, station, or base alerts on every passing bird or fails to detect a real incursion. When the threshold is low, the score does not have to be very high in order to prompt a positive classification by the system. The bar for marking an example positive is low. As the threshold gets higher, encountering examples that meet this higher standard becomes rarer and rarer. We can see an example in Figure 3.1, where the recall falls and the specificity rises as the threshold increases.[17]

Because different metrics imply different relative values for positive and negative examples, they will imply that different thresholds for positive classification are optimal. Figure 3.2 depicts this choice, plotting the summary metrics discussed so far against the total percentage

---

[16] Other techniques can be used to tune classifiers between these two extremes even when the classifier does not utilize scores in its determination. These techniques include resampling, which refers to adjusting the statistical properties of the training data (see, e.g., N. V. Chawla, K. W. Bowyer, L. O. Hall, and W. P. Kegelmeyer, "SMOTE: Synthetic Minority Over-Sampling Technique," *JAIR*, Vol. 16, June 1, 2002) and the use of "weights" to assign additional importance to either positive or negative examples (see, e.g., Yang Gu and Gondy Leroy, "Use of Conventional Machine Learning to Optimize Deep Learning Hyper-Parameters for NLP Labeling Tasks." *Proceedings of the 53rd Hawaii International Conference on System Sciences*, 2020). In general, if one wants to adjust a classifier's willingness to mark an example as positive, there are techniques that can be used to accomplish this.

[17] The data depicted in Figures 3.1 and 3.2 are collected from a score-based classifier trained to serve as a demonstration. Further detail can be found in the appendix.

**Figure 3.1**
**True Positive Rate and True Negative Rate Versus Threshold for a**
**Demonstration Classifier**

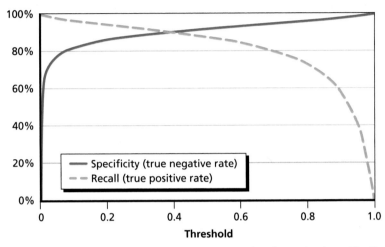

NOTE: This graph depicts data from a demonstration classifier trained specifically to illustrate metrics in this report. See appendix for more details.

**Figure 3.2**
**Some Metrics of Performance for the Demonstration Classifier Versus the**
**Total Proportion of Examples Marked Positive**

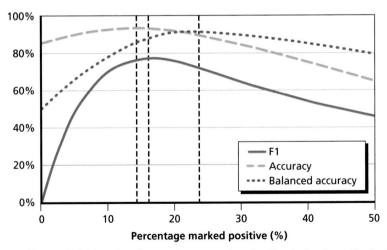

NOTE: This graph depicts data from a demonstration classifier trained specifically to illustrate metrics in this report. See appendix for more details.

of examples marked positive. Since decreasing the threshold results in a greater proportion of the examples being marked positive, this is in one-to-one correspondence with thresholds but easier to interpret on this plot. Each exhibits a clear maximum, obviously the optimal choice for the threshold *with respect to that metric.* The three maxima do not agree as to which threshold is optimal, occurring as they do at different thresholds. Thus, depending on the relative value one assigns to positive and negative examples (through choice of metric), one should choose a different strategy with respect to the willingness of the system to mark an example as positive (through, e.g., choice of threshold).

## Information Prioritization Performance Model

In this section we offer a quantitative model that provides a way of connecting the performance of an information prioritization system to its impacts, as measured by the resources devoted to using the system and the resulting risk of a missed detection. This model will be directly applicable only to binary classifiers and will make some simplifying assumptions about the deployment context of this system, particularly the operational tempo at which the system will be utilized. Even at this level of simplicity, we will see that the model can serve as a useful guide for connecting system properties to system impacts for system users and a way to understand the consequences of changing thresholds for classification. As we will discuss below, this model also serves as a useful starting point for more sophisticated models adapted to a particular real-world system.

For these systems, some progress can be made on rigorously and quantitatively assessing impact even at the level of abstraction at which the system categories are conceived. To ascertain what the impact of errors in a system that directs analyst attention is, we should ask what the impact of misdirecting analyst attention is. In the context of binary classifiers, this corresponds to asking what a false positive and a false negative mean for an analyst using the system. A false positive represents a waste of time: The system flags some artifact for review that, upon review, turns out to not assist the analyst with their job. This error can be treated as using up a portion of a budget of a constrained resource, user time, without providing any return on that investment. At first glance, this seems easily quantified. A false negative, however, is more challenging to trace to an impact. A false negative represents a missed opportunity for the user to interact with useful information. This could be a report that the analyst does not see and so does not make it into the analyst's product. How much does the absence of this one report affect the product written by the analyst? How much does the difference in the product move decisionmakers?

This issue can be sidestepped by analyzing false positives and false negatives differently. That is, the performance of the AI system can be viewed as determining the residual risk, or the overall number of false negatives, as a function of the resources invested to minimize that risk, or the amount of time a user spends reviewing the output of the system. If the user is willing to spend more time looking for useful pieces of information, the user will always find more useful items (or miss fewer, in the above formulation). The performance of the system sets the return on investment for this time. That is, does looking at twice as many items double the number of useful things one can expect to find, triple it, or increase it by a factor of one and a half?

When analyzing a concrete system, this allows us to calculate the level of risk (i.e., the number of items missed) that a given system produces as a function of the number of items that will actually be reviewed in practice. Alternatively, this can be used to derive the amount of review capacity required to reach a certain specified level of risk. Since each of these two calculations presents a single goal, either minimize risk or minimize resources needed, we can also use this framework to optimize classification thresholds according to either goal.

To accomplish this, the model considers the time an analyst has to review reports or raw data in a given day and the number of reports or pieces of raw data that arrive for review. We assume, given the aforementioned data glut experienced by intelligence analysts, that the latter exceeds the capacity of the former. Some of these reports will be useful to the analysts' set of assigned tasks, and others will not be. What the analyst must do is find the useful items and review them. As a simplifying assumption, we assume that the analyst has no helpful signals from the items themselves on which to base a guess as to which items are useful and must therefore choose completely at random.[18] The information prioritization system we seek to analyze helps in this task by providing a binary useful/not useful label to every item. Of course, this system is not perfect and will make errors, sometimes recommending items to the analyst that are not actually useful or failing to recommend important items. However, the analyst can expect to find more useful items this way than unassisted and so reviews items marked as useful before reviewing any marked as not useful, choosing randomly when necessary.[19] Under these assumptions, the model calculates how many useful items the analyst will find as a function of the number of items that arrive, the proportion that are actually useful, the proportion the analyst can review, and the properties (e.g., recall and specificity) of the system. See Figure 3.3 for a schematic depiction.

It might be clarifying to think of the model as operating on three categories of information—namely, information about the data, the system, and the deployment. Within each category, the model considers

- **Data:** How many items arrive per day? What percentage of them are useful?
- **System:** What is the performance of the classifier?[20]
- **Deployment:** What percentage of the items will be examined per day? What percentage of useful items will be found?

The model allows us to solve for exactly one of these quantities in terms of the others. Most frequently, we will be solving for one of the two

---

[18] This assumption is certainly not true in practice, but it does simplify the mathematics. More simplifying assumptions of this sort will follow shortly. While higher fidelity models can be built (see Directions for Generalization later in this chapter), even at this level the model illustrates the mechanisms that drive the effectiveness of an information prioritization system and more closely connect to concrete impacts than existing metrics.

[19] That is, if the system marks more items as useful than the analyst can review, the analyst chooses randomly among them. If the system marks fewer items as useful, the marked not-useful items the analyst reviews when they are done with those marked useful are chosen at random.

[20] This is specified in terms of any pair of the four metrics from Table 3.1. See Metrics for Binary Classifiers above for discussion on the sufficiency of this pair.

**Figure 3.3**
**Schematic Depiction of Information Prioritization Performance Mode**

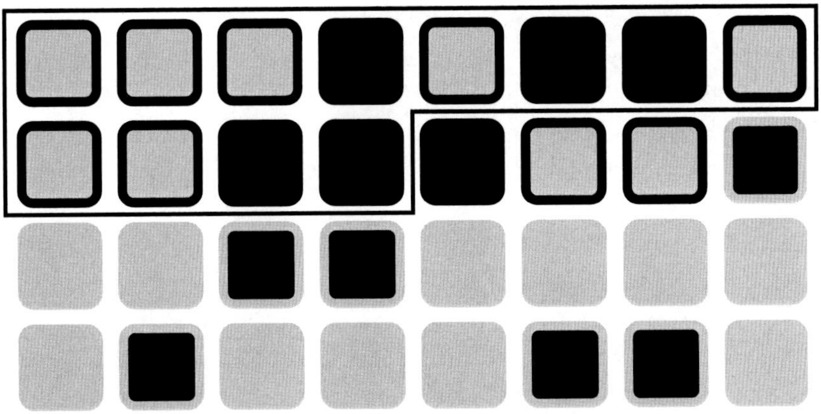

NOTE: Each square represents an individual item on which the system operates and that the analyst might review. The border color represents the determination of the classifier, and the interior color represents the truth, with black denoting useful, and gray denoting useless. So, for example, a black border with a gray interior represents a false positive. The box represents the subset of the items that the analyst will review. Note that there are more items marked useful than the analyst can review, so the analyst chooses among those marked useful.

deployment quantities, usually what percentage of useful items will be found.

### An Artificial Demonstration Scenario

In order to make this discussion more concrete and demonstrate the utility of this approach, we offer a simple vignette demonstrating the inputs and outputs to the model. Though the scenario we construct is entirely artificial, it shows what the model calculates and how it might inform strategy around whether to deploy a given system and how to devote resources to system utilization.

Thus, consider a hypothetical imagery analyst who on average receives 10,000 images conceivably related to their remit every day, but has the time to review only 100 when all of their duties are taken into account. For the purposes of applying the model, we must know how many images per day would contain useful information on average. In this example, we will assume ten images per day contain useful information. Without the aid of an information prioritization system, we can calculate that the expected number of useful images per day found by the analyst will be 0.1. Or, more concretely, we can expect the analyst to find one useful image every ten days.

Suppose that we have two systems that we can deploy to help the analyst; their properties are given in Table 3.2. As displayed in that table, we have two different questions we can ask of the model. The first question is: if the analyst devotes the same amount of resources to reviewing images (i.e., reviews 100 images every day), how many useful images will be found? We will call this a "fixed-resource deployment." Alternatively, we may have been comfortable with the efficacy of the analyst before we deployed the system. Perhaps finding one useful image every ten days is entirely sufficient for the mission with which this analyst is tasked. In this case, we might ask: how many images does the analyst have to look at in order to match their performance without the system? We call this a "fixed-impact deployment." More generally, we could vary the number of images reviewed freely after deployment and are not obligated to choose these two points. However, examining these two points can help demonstrate that we face a trade between the resources invested and the impact achieved.

System 1 represents a significant improvement over the status quo. If the analyst examines 100 images per day chosen with the assistance of the model, they can expect to find three useful images every day, a 30-fold improvement over unassisted searching. Conversely, the analyst must examine only 3.3 images every day (perhaps more easily parsed as ten images every three days) to match their previous perfor-

**Table 3.2**
**Artificial Model Demonstration**

|  | Recall | Specificity | Accuracy | Fixed-Resource | Fixed-Impact |
|---|---|---|---|---|---|
| System 1 | 62% | 98% | 98% | 3 images found | 3.3 images examined |
| System 2 | 10% | 99% | 99% | 1 image found | 10 images examined |

NOTE: Systems are notional and do not represent any real system.

mance while expending the minimal effort. In keeping with the theme that metric choice is nontrivial and metrics can disagree, System 2 performs less well when measured by these impact-derived metrics (one image found using System 2 versus three found using System 1, for example) despite possessing the higher accuracy (see Table 3.2).

### General Features of the Model

As alluded to in the previous section, one might also target a system deployment with a specified amount of resources that is devoted to reviewing the output of the system and that is not equal to the amount presently devoted to the task or to the amount required to match previous performance. In the above example, we might decide that we would like to distribute the gains of the system both to reducing the amount of time the analyst spends reviewing imagery and finding a greater proportion of useful imagery, say by having the analyst review only 50 images per day. How many images is the analyst expected to find, then?

The performance model is, in itself, agnostic as to how many images were being reviewed before deployment of the system. It is simply an equation for how many useful images are expected to be found using the information prioritization system as a function of how many images are reviewed. Therefore, the effectiveness of the classifier as judged by the information prioritization performance model is captured by a whole curve rather than a single number. One such curve for a notional system can be seen in Figure 3.4.[21] That is, for the *same* AI system different review capacities result in a different number that captures performance (i.e., a different percentage of useful items found). Therefore, the information prioritization performance model does not provide a single metric that captures the effectiveness of an information prioritization system but rather furnishes a *family* of metrics indexed by the percentage of the items that arrive each day and will be reviewed relative to the total number that arrive.

Though perhaps unexpected, the piecewise linear shape of this curve is intuitive in retrospect. On the left side of the curve, the analyst

---

[21] For more detail on what form these performance curves can take, see the appendix.

is still reviewing reports that the system has flagged as useful. There is a fixed chance (i.e., the precision) that any given report marked useful is in fact useful, so the number of useful reports found grows linearly in the number examined with slope equal to the precision. At a certain point, however, the analyst runs out of reports marked useful to review and must start reviewing reports marked as not useful. At this point, the corner in Figure 3.4, the slope decreases because a different and lower proportion of these items (one minus the negative predictive value) is in fact useful.

Recalling the discussion from the section on "Metrics for Binary Classifiers," we see that each of these metrics represents a distinct judgment as to the relative value of positive and negative examples. In this case, this judgment flows from a concrete reality of the deployment situation: As review capacity increases, more false positives can be tolerated in the service of surfacing more true positives, since review capacity becomes less scarce. Nonetheless, in situations where one classifier has better performance on positive examples and another has better performance on negative examples, which system is performing better overall should generally be expected to depend on the review capac-

**Figure 3.4**
**Percentage Found Versus Percentage Reviewed for a Notional System**

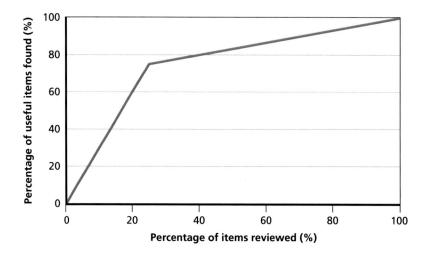

ity, just as preference between any such pair of classifiers should be expected to depend on the metric chosen.

Since each review capacity gives rise to a different metric, the optimal balance between false positives and false negatives for the classifier will depend on the review capacity through this metric, as discussed in the section on "Metrics for Binary Classifiers." Concretely, in the case of score-based classifiers, the optimal threshold for the classifier will depend on the number of items that can be reviewed. In and of itself, this fact is important to consider when managing the deployment of an information prioritization system, since changes in the review capacity devoted to using the system (e.g., resulting from budgetary changes or changes in analyst responsibilities) necessitate a different threshold to optimally utilize analyst time. Thus, changes in the system utilization may necessitate retuning the system.

As discussed in more detail in the appendix, under a relatively mild assumption the optimal threshold takes a simple and intuitive form: The information prioritization system should be optimized to return exactly as many items as can be reviewed every day. Essentially, this is due to the fact that returning either more or less than the number of items the analyst can review is a waste. If more items are returned than the analyst can review, chances are the pool has a lower proportion of useful items that it would have had if the system had been choosier and returned only as many as the analyst can review. On the other hand, if the system returns fewer items than the analyst can review, the analyst eventually has to examine items beyond those returned by the system in order to fill their time, thereby basically losing the help of the system for a portion of the task at hand.

Optimizing the threshold for each review capacity produces a new curve of how many reports will be found by the analyst as a function of how many can be reviewed where the performance at each point is the performance using the optimal threshold for that review capacity. This curve for the demonstration classifier is depicted in Figure 3.5 along with an arbitrarily chosen curve for a particular fixed threshold for comparison. This curve represents a useful ingredient for a decisionmaker when making investment decisions in the utilization of an information prioritization system. The x-axis, the review percentage,

**Figure 3.5**
**Percentage of Useful Items Found as a Function of Review Capacity**

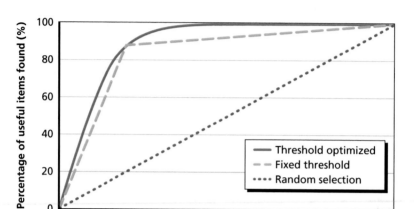

can be converted into the resource that it represents, such as analyst time or percentage of department budget. By considering what items the system serves to prioritize (e.g., images or SIGINT reports), decisionmakers can develop an understanding of what sort of risks are implied by missing 20 percent, 50 percent, or 80 percent of the items that are actually useful. Armed with this knowledge, decisionmakers can decide how many resources to devote to utilizing the system with an understanding of what risks and benefits attend to that decision. For example, looking at the system depicted in Figure 3.5, a decisionmaker might elect to allocate resources to review 20 percent of the incoming items every day using the system since a roughly 90-percent chance of catching any given useful item is sufficient, and obtaining a rough certainty of catching such an item would require doubling the resources allocated to utilizing the system.

**Taking Stock**

The information prioritization performance model represents a step forward in assessing the performance of systems that direct the attention of their user. This step forward was enabled by carefully analyzing the consequences of errors in the system and noticing that they are different primarily in kind rather than in magnitude. In a sense, the system spends a fixed budget of false positives, representing a fixed budget of user time, in order to minimize its false negatives, representing missed detections. This gives rise to ways of measuring the performance of these systems that do not attempt to conflate the consequences of the two errors by assigning them net value and sidesteps the difficult question of determining what the impact of a false negative is. This measure of performance is more closely related to the true effectiveness of the system and enables both more informed strategy about the value of the system in question and a more informed approach to optimizing the system for its task.

Of course, there is still work to be done and effects that should be captured in future studies. In reality, "usefulness" is not a binary variable but a spectrum. Two intelligence reports might both be useful, though one is absolutely critical and the other is simply informative. Similarly, the analyst cannot be expected to analyze precisely the same number of items every day, nor should we expect all items to take the same amount of time. For that matter, the analyst likely has some ability to understand what the content of a report is without reading it in its entirety, which conflicts with our assumption that the analyst chooses completely at random.[22] As it stands, the model is also not well optimized to characterize the effectiveness of warning systems. Though the warning function is squarely an information prioritization function (in that it directs attention to some emergent and important matter), many warnings do not come in batches in the way envisioned by the model. For example, a cyber intrusion detection system would likely raise a warning whenever it determined there was likely an intrusion.

---

[22] It should be noted, though, that the analyst must allocate a non-zero amount of time to a report in order to make a judgment as to the report's utility without the assistance of the system.

# CHAPTER FOUR

# Conclusions

## Key Findings

A clear criterion for what success looks like is critical for understanding both how close one has come and how to move closer to unambiguous success. In the case of AI systems, this definition must include some number of measured properties of the system's metrics, which summarize system performance. At present, although the AI and ML communities have a number of metrics for characterizing the performance of these systems, these metrics are frequently opaque and are not clearly connected with outcomes of interest in the context of intelligence.

In order to mitigate the opacity of existing metrics, we have offered a brief primer that details the methodology that underlies these metrics and gives a brief description of what a subset of them, those that characterize the performance of binary classifiers, actually measure. In order to attempt to connect these metrics with outcomes of interest to decisionmakers in intelligence analysis, we introduced a conceptual framework categorizing these systems by the way their output is utilized. For two of these categories, evaluation support and automated analysis, we found that characterizing the outcomes and impact that flow from the deployment of an AI system in that category is entangled with the question of assessing the overall impact of the intelligence process, which complicates a simple model of system effectiveness. For the remaining two, collection support and information prioritization, we identified ways to characterize the effectiveness of these systems that insulate them from these questions. For one of these, the category of information prioritization systems, we built and analyzed a simple quantitative model of how system properties create impacts.

In addition to providing the means to connect basic metrics characterizing the performance of an information prioritization binary classifier to the actual effectiveness of this system in terms of time savings and increase in capacity, the information prioritization performance model, together with the general discussion of metrics in machine learning, illustrates two general lessons:

- **Using metrics not matched to actual priorities obscures system performance and impedes informed choice of the optimal system.** Metrics are not necessarily meaningful in a vacuum, and decisionmakers should anticipate needing to do work to develop ways of measuring system performance that match their priorities. Since the metrics typically used to capture the performance of a system do not all agree on which of a pair of systems is performing better, simply choosing a metric arbitrarily will not enable decisionmakers to rank systems by how useful they will be to the mission the system supports. Similarly, engineering decisions ranging from overall model design to the optimization of the trade between false positives and false negatives are made to maximize system performance with respect to the metric of record. Metric choice should take place *before* the system is built and be guided by attempts to estimate the real impact of system deployment.

- **Effectiveness, and therefore the metrics that measure it, can depend not just on system properties, but on how the system is used.** In the case of information prioritization systems, this is captured by the dependence of the number of useful items found on the amount of time an analyst spends reviewing the output of the system. Since the optimal system is necessarily the most effective, this also means that which system is optimal can depend on how the system is used. In the context of information prioritization systems, this manifests in the fact that different review percentages can result in different determinations as to which of a pair of systems is preferable. That is, for a given pair of systems, which system is more effective can depend on how much of the system output can be reviewed. On an engineering level, this affects the optimal trade-off between false positives and false negatives. However, both for the question of understanding the effectiveness of a system and that of choosing the optimal system, these are simply examples of more general lessons. When deploying a system, decisionmakers should understand that choices about how the system is used may affect outcomes in concert with the properties of the system itself. Chief among these is the amount of resources devoted to the mission *outside* those devoted to building the system.

## Recommendations for the Intelligence Community

**Begin with the right metrics.** When considering acquiring an AI system, DoD and the IC should begin by developing a detailed understanding of the way this system will be utilized and choosing metrics that reflect success with respect to this utilization. For information prioritization systems in particular, we recommend a version of the information prioritization performance model, possibly adapted and extended to cover the precise case at hand. Through this process, system acquirers can understand what the impact of the performance achieved by system designers will be. System designers will also benefit from the clear objective guiding their engineering decisions and will deliver a more effective system if this objective is aligned with user priorities.

**Reevaluate (and retune) regularly.** Since the world around the system continues to evolve after deployment, system evaluation must continue as a portion of regular maintenance. Narrowly, this means continuing to assemble test data and measure the performance of the system to detect any changes in performance. More broadly, this must include reevaluations of the deployment context of the system. Is the system still being used in the way first envisioned when it was deployed? Is the same amount of resources being devoted to utilizing the output of the system and accomplishing the mission the system is meant to support? As these details change, the right way to measure effectiveness may shift. At the most dramatic, this might result in entirely different metrics from those that were used to evaluate the system at deployment becoming most appropriate. In addition, the system might need to be retuned, for example, to a different balance between false positives and false negatives, to reflect the changing priorities of users.

**Speak the language.** System designers have a well-established set of metrics typically used to capture the performance of AI systems. Though new metrics can be constructed, being conversant in these traditional metrics will ease communication with experts during the process of designing a new system or maintaining an existing one. Ensure that coursework for acquisition professionals who may acquire AI systems provides an introduction to these traditional metrics. Additionally, acquisition professionals would benefit from an understanding of the assumptions and reasoning that underlie the statistical approach to evaluating these systems, which could also be included in the relevant coursework. More broadly, a common resource on metrics for AI systems should be created or identified that can serve as a common touchpoint across the IC.

**Conduct further research into methods of evaluating AI system effectiveness.** In addition to representing a step forward for assessing the effectiveness of AI systems supporting intelligence, this effort serves as a demonstration of what is lost when well-tuned methods of assessing this effectiveness are not present. Unfortunately, further basic research is needed to provide these methods across all the systems and deployment contexts pertinent to intelligence missions. This research is distinct from the considerable effort rightly directed toward developing methodologies for assuring the integrity and reliability of AI systems for defense and intelligence applications.[1] In addition to being able to assure that these systems will not suddenly stop working at a critical juncture, we must be able to critically assess whether they will enhance effectiveness in the mission they support at

---

[1]  See, e.g., Andrew J. Lohn, "Estimating the Brittleness of AI: Safety Integrity Levels and the Need for Testing Out-of-Distribution Performance," Cornell University arXiv, preprint arXiv: 2009.00802, 2020.

all when judged not just by a narrow definition of their task but by the actual value they provide. Put another way, research is needed to actually understand the contours of the upside for such systems, in addition to understanding how to guard against downsides. At present, for intelligence in particular, the results of this effort indicate that room for improvement remains in methodologies for assessing the actual value provided to users by these systems.

# Derivations and Technical Details

This appendix gives additional detail on some of the arguments and methods discussed in the main report for the benefit of the more technical segment of the audience, who may be curious about the structure of the arguments or interested in adapting them for their own use case. We open with a brief discussion of the mathematical underpinnings of some of the discussion on the metrics for binary classifiers and then move to a presentation of the information prioritization performance model.

## Measuring the Performance of a Binary Classifier

Assuming the classification decisions are independent of one another, the performance of a binary classifier is captured by the statistical relationship between two binary variables, $Z$, the label assigned by the classifier; and $Y$, the true label. As noted in the main text, the two possible outcomes for each of these variables gives rise to four mutually exclusive possible outcomes for the classification decision. Therefore, at most four numbers, namely $P(Z = 1, Y = 1)$, $P(Z = 1, Y = 0)$, $P(Z = 0, Y = 1)$, and $P(Z = 0, Y = 0)$, are needed to fully capture the performance of the classifier. Since these numbers are the probability of four mutually exclusive, exhaustive events, they must sum to 1:

$$P(Z = 1, Y = 1) + P(Z = 1, Y = 0) + P(Z = 0, Y = 1) + P(Z = 0, Y = 0) = 1.$$

This one constraint means that at most, three numbers are needed to capture the performance of the classifier. However, one of these three numbers is not a property of the classifier but of the underlying data: The marginal probability of the true label does not depend on the performance of the classifier at all. From the point of view of distinguishing among the performance of different classifiers on the same data, the equation for this marginal probability,

$$P(Y = 1) = P(Z = 1, Y = 1) + P(Z = 0, Y = 1),$$

can be regarded as a second constraint on the four numbers capturing classifier performance.

The remaining two degrees of freedom can be reparametrized as

$$P(Z = 1 \mid Y = 1) = \frac{P(Z = 1, Y = 1)}{P(Y = 1)}$$

and

$$P(Z = 0 \mid Y = 0) = \frac{P(Z = 0, Y = 0)}{P(Y = 0)},$$

which are clearly properties of the variable $Z$ and thus properties of the classifier. The first of these two can be recognized as the recall and the second as the specificity. Thus, the space of possible classifiers for a given set of data is parametrized by two numbers between 0 and 1.[1]

These two numbers are sufficient to characterize the performance, up to any invertible reparameterization. Provided that any reparameterization is increasing in both specificity and recall, that reparameterization will also preserve the order of preferences where a universal preference exists between a pair of classifiers. However, as noted in the main report, the fact that there are two separate degrees of freedom for classifier performance means that even with the assumption that higher recall and higher specificity must both be preferable, there are ambiguous cases where no universal preference exists between pairs of classifiers. Choosing a metric certainly adjudicates these cases, as the

---

[1]  For additional discussion and a different perspective, see Flach, 2003.

metric induces a preference relation on the two-dimensional space of classifier performances. A theorem of microeconomics gives the converse, provided that the preference relation is continuous, and higher specificity and recall are preferred to lower.[2]

## The Information Prioritization Performance Model

Recall that in this model, we assume that the information prioritization system marks every item as useful or not useful and that the analyst then reviews a fixed number of the items chosen based only on the label assigned by the system. For compactness of notation, write $r = P(Y = 1)$, $p_1 = P(Z = 1 | Y = 1)$, and $p_0 = P(Z = 0 | Y = 0)$. For simplicity, we assume that the number of items arriving in the period of analysis, $n$, is Poisson distributed with mean $N$. We denote the number of documents that the analyst can review by $M$. Provided that

$$p_1 > 1 - p_0,$$

then the first-order stochastic dominant strategy is for the analyst to review items marked useful (i.e., positives) before those marked useless. In the case of equality, all strategies are equivalent to random guessing. If the inequality is reversed, then an item marked useless is actually more likely to be useful than one marked useful, and the labels on the classifier should be reversed, reversing the inequality.

The expected number of items found, $\mathbb{E}[f]$, simplifies somewhat in the limit of large $N$ with fixed $M/N$. Though working in this limit is a limitation of this work, we expect that this limit is the most relevant to the applications envisioned, since these systems are necessary only when there is a great deal of data to sift through. With the stated assumptions, this is due to the fact that the Poisson distribution is asymptotically Gaussian in this regime with a variance that grows linearly in the mean. We suspect that this result depends only on

2   G. A. Jehle and P. J. Reny. *Advanced Microeconomic Theory*, 3rd ed., Essex: Pearson Education Limited, 2011, Theorem 1.1.

the variance of $n$ growing more slowly than $N^2$, though. In this limit, we have

$$\mathbb{E}[f] \approx p_1 M \Theta\left(1 - \frac{M}{\lambda N}\right) + \left[(1 - p_0)(M - \lambda N) + p_1 r N\right]\Theta\left(\frac{M}{\lambda N} - 1\right), \quad (A.1)$$

where $\Theta$ denotes the Heavyside step function,

$$\lambda = p_1 r + (1 = p_0)(1 - r)$$

is the percentage of the items that are marked positive,

$$p_1 = \frac{p_1 r}{\lambda}$$

is the precision, and

$$p_0 = \frac{p_0(1 - r)}{1 - \lambda}$$

is the negative predictive value.

Figure A.1 gives an example of the shape of $\mathbb{E}[f]$ as a function of $M$, scaled as $\mathbb{E}[f]/_{rN}$ plotted against $M/_N$. This is precisely the return-on-investment curve alluded to in the main report. Per Equation A.1, this curve can be seen to be piecewise linear in $M/_N$. It is likely easiest to think of this curve as being controlled by the point $x = \lambda$, $y = p_1$, since the curve will always consist of two line segments: one from (0,0) to this point, and one from this point to (1,1). The first line segment, connecting (0,0) to the point that controls the curve, gives the performance while the analyst is reviewing items that were marked useful by the system. This explains why the slope in this region is the precision, $p_1$: The chance that a marginal additional item examined by the analyst will be useful is the chance that a randomly chosen item marked useful by the system will in fact be useful. At the controlling point, the slope changes since the useful items have been exhausted, and the chance that a marginal item will be useful is one minus the negative predictive value.

**Figure A.1**
**Annotated Performance of a Notional System**

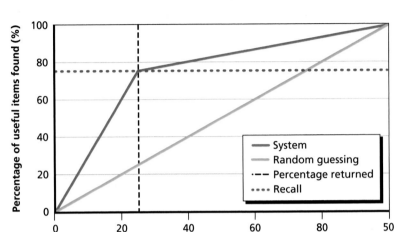

Figure A.2 demonstrates how the shape of this curve changes as the properties of the classifier change. Increasing the recall with fixed precision affords a larger window of $M/N$ for the percentage found to grow at the initial slope, moving the controlling point up along the ini-

**Figure A.2**
**Demonstration of the Effect of System Performance on Effectiveness**

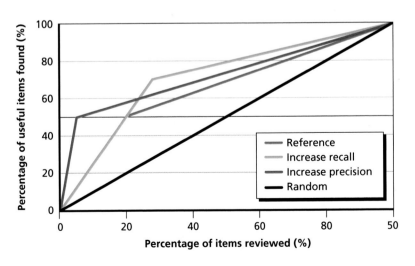

tial slope. Increasing the precision with fixed recall, on the other hand, slides the point leftward at a fixed height, because the system reaches the height at which the slope changes, that is, the recall, more rapidly due to the increased slope. This figure also demonstrates the effect alluded to in the main report: Since each review percentage gives rise to a different summary metric, which classifier is preferable can depend on the review percentage. In this figure, the classifier with greater precision is preferable at lower review percentages, while the classifier with greater recall is preferable at higher review percentages. This is generally true of any pair of classifiers between which the preference is ambiguous.

As with any metric, some threshold must be optimal with respect to the number of useful items found at any fixed percentage of items reviewed. Figure A.3 explores the relationship between the threshold (as captured by the percentage of the items that are marked positive, $\lambda$) and the percentage of items that will be reviewed by the analyst. The figure is the analog of Figure 3.2, but with the compared metrics defined by different review percentages. Figure A.3 demonstrates that

**Figure A.3**
**Demonstration of Classifier Percentage Found Versus Percentage Returned**

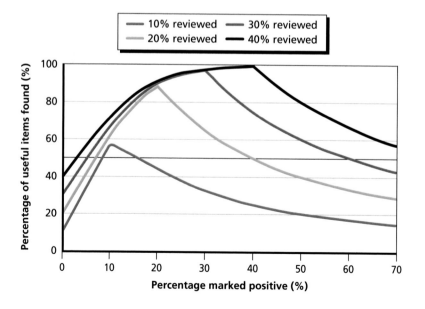

proper choice of threshold can make a dramatic difference in the performance of an information prioritization system. For example, with a review percentage of 40 percent, the demonstration classifier achieves percentages found ranging from 40 percent to nearly 100 percent, depending on how close to optimally the threshold is set. This figure also strongly suggests a general result: The optimal threshold matches the percentage returned by the system to the percentage that can be reviewed.

To explore the conditions under which this is true, rewrite Equation A.1 as

$$\phi \approx \phi_1 \Theta \left( 1 - \frac{\mu}{\lambda} \right) + \phi_0 \Theta \left( \frac{\mu}{\lambda} - 1 \right), \tag{A.2}$$

where

$$\phi = \frac{\mathbb{E}[f]}{rN}$$

$$\mu = \frac{M}{N}$$

$$\phi_1 = p_1 \frac{\mu}{\lambda},$$

and

$$\phi_0 = 1 - \left( 1 - p_1 \right) \frac{1 - \mu}{1 - \lambda}.$$

If $p_1$ is strictly concave in $\lambda$,

$$\frac{d^2 p_1}{d\lambda^2} < 0,$$

then using the fact that $p_1$ must lie below its tangents, one can show that

$$\frac{d\phi_0}{d\lambda} > 0 \ and \ \frac{d\phi_1}{d\lambda} < 0,$$

which implies that $\phi$ reaches a maximum at $\lambda = \mu$, giving the result that the system should return precisely as many items as the analyst will review. Evaluating Equation A.2 at this point shows that the opti-mal number found is then simply the recall, $p_1$.

Inspecting Figure 3.5, which plots the recall against the percentage returned in the guise of the number found, we see that the demonstration classifier is clearly strictly concave. The requirement that the recall be strictly concave is not as restrictive as it might initially seem, since techniques exist to "repair" regions of convexity in this function by building "hybrid" classifiers out of classifiers that exist around the region of convexity.[3] Though the requirement for strict concavity should be kept in mind, it is unlikely to be limiting in practice.

## Demonstration Classifier

The demonstration classifier used was a BERT-based natural language classifier trained by fine-tuning the pretrained BERT model distributed with the "transformers" python module using the methodology laid out in the original paper on the Quora Question Pairs dataset, a portion of the GLUE natural language benchmark.[4] The results shown are derived from the scores this classifier assigned to the development set. To render some of the effects more easily seen on the graphs, we conducted subsequent analysis as if the prevalence of the positive class was 15 percent rather than the approximately 37 percent implied by the distribution of the development set.

---

[3]  Foster Provost and Tom Fawcett, "Robust Classification for Imprecise Environments," *Machine Learning*, Vol. 42, No. 3 (2001); Peter A. Flach and Shaomin Wu, "Repairing Concavities in ROC Curves," *IJCAI*, 2005.

[4]  Devlin et al., 2018; Wang et al., 2019.

# Bibliography

Altman, Douglas G., and J. Martin Bland, "Statistics Notes: Diagnostic Tests 2: Predictive Values," *BMJ*, Vol. 309, No. 6947, 1994. As of September 30, 2020: https://www.bmj.com/content/309/6947/102.1

Breiman, Leo, "Statistical Modeling: The Two Cultures (with Comments and a Rejoinder by the Author)," *Statistical Science*, Vol. 16, No. 3, 2001, pp. 199–231. As of September 10, 2020: https://projecteuclid.org/euclid.ss/1009213726

Brin, Sergey, and Lawrence Page, "The Anatomy of a Large-Scale Hypertextual Web Search Engine." *Computer Networks and ISDN Systems*, 30.1–7, 1998, pp. 107–117.

Casella, George, and Roger L. Berger, *Statistical Inference*, Vol. 2, Pacific Grove, Calif.: Duxbury, 2002.

Chapman, Lizette, "Palantir Wins New Pentagon Deal with $111 Million from the Army," Bloomberg, December 13, 2019. As of September 19, 2020: https://www.bloomberg.com/news/articles/2019-12-14/palantir-wins-new -pentagon-deal-with-111-million-from-the-army

Chawla, N. V., K. W. Bowyer, L. O. Hall, and W. P. Kegelmeyer, "SMOTE: Synthetic Minority Over-Sampling Technique," *JAIR*, Vol. 16, June 1, 2002, pp. 321–357. As of September 20, 2020: https://www.jair.org/index.php/jair/article/view/10302

Devlin, Jacob, Ming-Wei Chang, Kenton Lee, and Kristina Toutanova, "BERT: Pre-Training of Deep Bidirectional Transformers for Language Understanding," Cornell University arXiv, 2018. As of September 9, 2020: https://arxiv.org/abs/1810.04805

Elkan, Charles, "The Foundations of Cost-Sensitive Learning," *Proceedings of the 17th International Joint Conference on Artificial Intelligence*, Vol. 2, August 2001, pp. 973–978. As of June 30, 2021: https://dl.acm.org/doi/10.5555/1642194.1642224

Ettinger, Jared, "Cyber Intelligence Tradecraft Report," Carnegie Mellon University, Software Engineering Institute, May 2019. As of September 16, 2020: https://resources.sei.cmu.edu/asset_files/Collection/2019_300_001_546590.pdf

Fawcett, Tom, "An Introduction to ROC Analysis," *Pattern Recognition Letters*, Vol. 27, No. 8, 2006, pp. 861–874. As of September 10, 2020: https://www.sciencedirect.com/science/article/pii/S016786550500303X

Flach, Peter A., "The Geometry of ROC Space: Understanding Machine Learning Metrics Through ROC Isometrics," *Proceedings of the 20th International Conference on Machine Learning (ICML-03)*, Washington, D.C., 2003. As of September 30, 2020: https://www.aaai.org/Papers/ICML/2003/ICML03-028.pdf

Flach, Peter A., and Shaomin Wu, "Repairing Concavities in ROC Curves," *IJCAI*, 2005. As of June 4, 2021: https://www.ijcai.org/Proceedings/05/Papers/0652.pdf

Friedman, Jerome, Trevor Hastie, and Robert Tibshirani, "The Elements of Statistical Learning," *Springer Series in Statistics*, Vol. 1, No. 10, 2001. As of September 9, 2020: https://web.stanford.edu/~hastie/Papers/ESLII.pdf

Gartin, Joseph W., "The Future of Analysis," *Studies in Intelligence*, Vol. 63. No. 2, Extracts, June 2019. As of April 1, 2021: https://www.cia.gov/static/8bdbc27e6a29bf09201ccdaf45677a61/Future-of -Analysis.pdf

Gu, Yang, and Gondy Leroy, "Use of Conventional Machine Learning to Optimize Deep Learning Hyper-parameters for NLP Labeling Tasks," *Proceedings of the 53rd Hawaii International Conference on System Sciences*, 2020. As of September 20, 2020: https://scholarspace.manoa.hawaii.edu/handle/10125/63867

IARPA—*See* Intelligence Advanced Research Projects Activity.

Intelligence Advanced Research Projects Activity, "Automated Low-Level Analysis and Description of Diverse Intelligence Video (ALADDIN) Broad Agency Announcement (BAA)," IARPA-BAA-10-01, June 28, 2010. As of September 20, 2020: https://beta.sam.gov/opp/0182a2b6e1976f7cf6e9d8c78dc378b8/view?keywords= iarpa-baa-10-01&sort=-relevance&index=&is_active=false&page=1&date_filter_ index=0&inactive_filter_values=false

————, "Open Source Indicators (OSI)," IARPA-BAA-11-11, August 23, 2011. As of April 1, 2021: https://www.iarpa.gov/index.php/research-programs/osi/baa

———, "Mercury Broad Agency Announcement," IARPA-BAA-15-08, June 12, 2015. As of September 20, 2020:
https://sam.gov/opp/a60fa9b0a0e3e5dfcaf2244e5f82691e/view?keywords=iarpa%20BAA-15-08&sort=-relevance&index=&is_active=false&page=1&date_filter_index=0&inactive_filter_values=false

———, "Cyber-Attack Automated Unconventional Sensor Environment (CAUSE)," IARPA-BAA-15-06, July 17, 2015. As of September 20, 2020:
https://www.iarpa.gov/index.php/research-programs/cause/cause-baa

———, "HFC Proposers Day Announcement," December 18, 2015. As of May 25, 2021:
https://www.iarpa.gov/images/files/programs/hfc/HFC%20Proposers%20Day.pdf

———, "MATERIAL PD Announcement," August 1, 2016. As of September 20, 2020:
https://www.iarpa.gov/index.php/research-programs/material/material-baa

———, "Hybrid Forecasting Competition (HFC)," BAA-16-02, September 12, 2016. As of April 1, 2021:
https://www.iarpa.gov/index.php/research-programs/hfc/hfc-baa

———, "Functional Genomic and Computational Assessment of Threats (Fun GCAT) Broad Agency Announcement," IARPA-BAA-16-08, September 22, 2016. As of September 20, 2020:
https://www.iarpa.gov/index.php/research-programs/fun-gcat/fun-gcat-baa

———, "Creation of Operationally Realistic 3D Environment (CORE3D) Broad Agency Announcement," IARPA-BAA-16-06, November 1, 2016. As of September 20, 2020:
https://www.iarpa.gov/index.php/research-programs/core3d/core3d-baa

———, "Deep Intermodal Video Analytics (DIVA) Broad Agency Announcement," IARPA-BAA-16-13, March 17, 2017. As of September 20, 2020:
https://www.iarpa.gov/index.php/research-programs/diva/diva-baa

———, "Finding Engineering-Linked Indicators (FELIX) Broad Agency Announcement," IARPA-BAA-17-07, August 31, 2017. As of September 20, 2020:
https://www.iarpa.gov/index.php/research-programs/felix/felix-baa

———, "Better Extraction from Text Towards Enhanced Retrieval (BETTER)," IARPA-BAA-18-05, September 28, 2018. As of September 20, 2020:
https://www.iarpa.gov/index.php/research-programs/better?id=1081

Ish, Daniel, Andrew M. Parker, Osonde A. Osoba, Marc N. Elliot, Mark Schlesinger, Ron D. Hays, Rachel Grob, Dale Shaller, and Steven C. Martino, *Using Natural Language Processing to Code Patient Experience Narratives: Capabilities and Challenges*, Santa Monica, Calif.: RAND Corporation, RR-A628-1, 2020. As of April 1, 2021:
https://www.rand.org/pubs/research_reports/RRA628-1.html

Jehle, G. A., and P. J. Reny, *Advanced Microeconomic Theory*, 3rd ed., Essex: Pearson Education Limited, 2011.

Johnston, Rob, "Analytic Culture in the US Intelligence Community, An Ethnographic Study," Washington, D.C.: CIA, Center for the Study of Intelligence, 2005. As of April 1, 2021:
https://fas.org/irp/cia/product/analytic.pdf

Joint Artificial Intelligence Center, "Joint Information Warfare," undated. As of April 1, 2021:
https://www.ai.mil/mi_joint_information_warfare.html

———, "The JCF and the Combatant Commands: A Symbiotic Relationship," *AI in Defense*, June 3, 2020. As of September 20, 2020:
https://www.ai.mil/blog_06_03_20-the_jcf_and_the_combatant_commands_a_symbiotic_relationship.html

Kaplan, Jared, Sam McCandlish, Tom Henighan, Tom B. Brown, Benjamin Chess, Rewon Child, Scott Gray, Alec Radford, Jeffrey Wu, and Dario Amodei, "Scaling Laws for Neural Language Models," Cornell University arXiv, 2020. As of September 10, 2020:
https://arxiv.org/abs/2001.08361

Keller, John, "Project Maven Moves to ABMS to Showcase Technologies in Artificial Intelligence (AI) and Machine Learning," *Military & Aerospace Electronics*, September 8, 2020. As of September 20, 2020:
https://www.militaryaerospace.com/computers/article/14182594/artificial-intelligence-ai-sensors-machine-learning

Li, Yuezun, and Siwei Lyu, "Exposing Deepfake Videos by Detecting Face Warping Artifacts," Cornell University arXiv, 2018. As of in September 9, 2020:
https://arxiv.org/abs/1811.00656

Liptak, Andrew, "Palmer Luckey's Company Earned a Contract for the Pentagon's Project Maven AI Program," *The Verge*, March 10, 2019. As of September 20, 2020:
https://www.theverge.com/2019/3/10/18258553/palmer-luckey-anduril-industries-pentagon-project-maven-ai-program-vr

Liu, Yi, Jialiang Peng, James J. Q Yu, and Yi Wu, "PPGAN: Privacy-Preserving Generative Adversarial Network," *2019 IEEE 25th International Conference on Parallel and Distributed Systems*, 2019.

Lohn, Andrew J., "Estimating the Brittleness of AI: Safety Integrity Levels and the Need for Testing Out-of-Distribution Performance," Cornell University arXiv, preprint arXiv: 2009.00802, 2020. As of April 1, 2021:
https://arxiv.org/abs/2009.00802

Lowenthal, Mark M., *Intelligence: From Secrets to Policy*, 8th ed., Washington, D.C.: Sage, Congressional Quarterly Press, 2020.

Metsis, Vangelis, Ion Androutsopoulos, and Georgios Paliouras, "Spam Filtering with Naive Bayes—Which Naive Bayes?" *CEAS*, Vol. 17, 2006. As of September 10, 2020:
http://www2.aueb.gr/users/ion/docs/ceas2006_paper.pdf

Metz, Cade, "In Two Moves, AlphaGo and Lee Sedol Redefined the Future," *Wired*, March 16, 2016. As of September 9, 2020:
https://www.wired.com/2016/03/two-moves-alphago-lee-sedol-redefined-future/

Mulchandani, Nand, Jane Pinelis, and Brad Boyd, "Joint Artificial Intelligence Center Leaders Update Reporters on DoD AI Developments," transcript, September 10, 2020. As of September 20, 2020:
https://www.defense.gov/Newsroom/Transcripts/Transcript/Article/2345500/joint-artificial-intelligence-center-leaders-update-reporters-on-dod-ai-develop/

Munoz, Carlo, "JAIC Smart Sensor Plays Key Role in USAF Advanced ISR Pod Prototype," *Janes*, September 21, 2020. As of September 21, 2020:
https://www.janes.com/defence-news/news-detail/jaic-smart-sensor-plays-key-role-in-usaf-advanced-isr-pod-prototype

Nakkiran, Preetum, Gal Kaplun, Yamini Bansal, Tristan Yang, Boaz Barak, and Ilya Sutskever, "Deep Double Descent: Where Bigger Models and More Data Hurt," Cornell University arXiv, 2019. As of September 9, 2020:
https://arxiv.org/abs/1912.02292

National Academies of Sciences, Engineering, and Medicine, *Implications of Artificial Intelligence for Cybersecurity: Proceedings of a Workshop*, Washington, D.C.: National Academies Press, 2019.

National Science and Technology Council, Select Committee on Artificial Intelligence, "The National Artificial Intelligence Research and Development Strategic Plan: 2019 Update," June 2019. As of April 1, 2021:
https://www.nitrd.gov/pubs/National-AI-RD-Strategy-2019.pdf

National Security Commission on Artificial Intelligence, "About," webpage, undated. As of September 22, 2020:
https://www.nscai.gov/about/about

———, "Second Quarter Recommendations," *Quarterly Series*, No. 2, July 2020, p. 108.

ODNI—*See* Office of the Director of National Intelligence.

Office of the Director of National Intelligence, "How the IC Works," webpage, undated a. As of April 1, 2021:
https://www.intelligence.gov/how-the-ic-works

———, "What Is Intelligence?" webpage, undated b. As of September 14, 2020:
https://www.dni.gov/index.php/what-we-do/what-is-intelligence

———, "Intelligence Community Directive 203: Analytic Standards," 2015.

———, "Processes for Assessing the Efficacy and Value of Intelligence Programs," February 8, 2016.

———, "The AIM Initiative: A Strategy for Augmenting Intelligence Using Machines," *ODNI Report*, January 16, 2019. As of April 1, 2021: https://www.dni.gov/index.php/newsroom/reports-publications/item/1940-the -aim-initiative-a-strategy-for-augmenting-intelligence-using-machines

———, "Artificial Intelligence Ethics Framework for the Intelligence Community," v. 1.0, June 2020. As of September 11, 2020: https://www.dni.gov/files/ODNI/documents/AI_Ethics_Framework_for_the_ Intelligence_Community_10.pdf

———, "Intelligence Community Releases Artificial Intelligence Principles and Framework," press release, July 23, 2020. As of September 11, 2020: https://www.dni.gov/index.php/newsroom/press-releases/item/2134-intelligence -community-releases-artificial-intelligence-principles-and-framework

Palantir Technologies, Form S-1/A, 2020. As of September 20, 2020: https://sec.report/Document/0001193125-20-241694/

Paswan, Mithilesh Kumar, P. Shanthi Bala, and G. Aghila. "Spam Filtering: Comparative Analysis of Filtering Techniques," *IEEE-International Conference on Advances in Engineering, Science and Management (ICAESM-2012)*, 2012. As of September 10, 2020: https://ieeexplore.ieee.org/document/6215593?arnumber=6215593&contentType= Conference%20Publications

Pomerleau, Mark, "Pentagon's AI Center to Field New Psychological Operations Tool," C4ISRNET, September 11, 2020. As of September 19, 2020: https://www.c4isrnet.com/artificial-intelligence/2020/09/11/pentagons-ai-center -to-field-new-psychological-operations-tool

Provost, Foster, and Tom Fawcett, "Robust Classification for Imprecise Environments," *Machine Learning*, Vol. 42, No. 3, 2001, pp. 203–231.

Remarks as Prepared for Robert Cardillo, Director National Geospatial-Intelligence Agency, June 5, 2017. As of April 1, 2021: https://www.nga.mil/news/GEOINT_2017_Symposium.html

Russakovsky, Olga, Jia Deng, Hao Su, Jonathan Krause, Sanjeev Satheesh, Sean Ma, Zhiheng Huang, Andrej Karpathy, Aditya Khosla, Michael Bernstein, Alexander C. Berg, and Li Fie-Fei, "ImageNet Large Scale Visual Recognition Challenge," *International Journal of Computer Vision*, Vol. 115, No. 3, 2015, pp. 211–252. As of September 8, 2020: https://arxiv.org/abs/1409.0575

Shalom, Y. Bar, and X. R. Li, *Multisensor, Multitarget Tracking: Principles and Techniques*, Storrs, Conn.: YBS, 1979.

Silver, David, Aja Huang, Chris J. Maddison, Arthur Guez, Laurent Sifre, George van den Driessche, Julian Schrittwieser, Ioannis Antonoglou, Veda Panneershelvam, Marc Lanctot, Sander Dieleman, Dominik Grewe, John Nham, Nal Kalchbrenner, Ilya Sutskever, Timothy Lillicrap, Madeleine Leach, Koray Kavukcuoglu, Thore Graepel, and Demis Hassabis, "Mastering the Game of Go with Deep Neural Networks and Tree Search," *Nature*, Vol. 529, No. 7587, 2016, pp. 484–489. As of September 20, 2020:
https://pubmed.ncbi.nlm.nih.gov/26819042/

Src, Inc., "Teraflops of Processing Power at 26,000 Feet," 2018. As of September 19, 2020:
https://www.srcinc.com/pdf/Whitepaper-Agile-Condor.pdf

Strout, Nathan, "Inside the Army's Futuristic Test of Its Battlefield Artificial Intelligence in the Desert," C4ISRNET, September 25, 2020. As of September 19, 2020:
https://www.c4isrnet.com/artificial-intelligence/2020/09/25/the-army-just
-conducted-a-massive-test-of-its-battlefield-artificial-intelligence-in-the-desert

Sutton, Richard S., and Andrew G. Barto, *Reinforcement Learning: An Introduction*, Cambridge, Mass.: MIT Press, 2018.

Tarraf, Danielle C., William Shelton, Edward Parker, Brien Alkire, Diana Gehlhaus, Justin Grana, Alexis Levedahl, Jasmin Leveille, Jared Mondschein, James Ryseff, Ali Wyne, Dan Elinoff, Edward Geist, Benjamin N. Harris, Eric Hui, Cedric Kenney, Sydne Newberry, Chandler Sachs, Peter Schirmer, Danielle Schlang, Victoria M. Smith, Abbie Tingstad, Padmaja Vedula, and Kristin Warren, *The Department of Defense Posture for Artificial Intelligence: Assessment and Recommendations*, Santa Monica, Calif.: RAND Corporation, RR-4229-OSD, 2019. As of October 15, 2020:
https://www.rand.org/pubs/research_reports/RR4229.html

Treverton, Gregory F., *Reshaping National Intelligence for an Age of Information*, New York: Cambridge University Press, 2003.

Trevithick, Joseph, "MQ-9 Reaper Flies with AI Pod That Sifts Through Huge Sums of Data to Pick Out Targets," *The Drive*, September 4, 2020. As of September 9, 2020:
https://www.thedrive.com/the-war-zone/36205/reaper-drone-flies-with-podded
-ai-that-sifts-through-huge-sums-of-data-to-pick-out-targets

Vincent, Brandi, "How the Pentagon's JAIC Says It's Prioritizing Ethics in Its AI-Driven Pursuits," Nextgov, September 10, 2020. As of September 9, 2020:
https://www.nextgov.com/emerging-tech/2020/09/
how-pentagons-jaic-says-its-prioritizing-ethics-its-ai-driven-pursuits/168386/

Wang, Alex, Amanpreet Singh, Julian Michael, Felix Hill, Omer Levy, and Samuel R Bowman, "Glue: A Multi-Task Benchmark and Analysis Platform for Natural Language Understanding," Cornell University arXiv, February 22, 2019. As of September 9, 2020:
https://arxiv.org/abs/1804.07461

Wolfe, Frank, "Testing Begins for Condor Pod to Enable AI-Powered MQ-9 Reaper Targeting," *Aviation Today*, September 14, 2020. As of September 9, 2020:
https://www.aviationtoday.com/2020/09/14/testing-begins-condor-pod-enable-ai-powered-mq-9-reaper-targeting